OLD HOUSE ECO HANDBOOK

A PRACTICAL GUIDE TO RETROFITTING FOR ENERGY-EFFICIENCY & SUSTAINABILITY

Marianne Suhr & Roger Hunt

In association with
THE SOCIETY FOR THE PROTECTION OF ANCIENT BUILDINGS

FRANCES LINCOLN

Dedication

For the generation who will inherit our successes as well as our mistakes
Charlie, Max and Ben MARIANNE SUHR
Nick, Annie, Kate and Eppie ROGER HUNT

In memory of Richard Valentine Cain 1965–2011
Exceptional draughtsman, gifted surveyor and a great ambassador for old buildings

Frances Lincoln Limited

www.franceslincoln.com

OLD HOUSE ECO HANDBOOK: A PRACTICAL GUIDE TO RETROFITTING
FOR ENERGY-EFFICIENCY & SUSTAINABILITY
Copyright © 2013 Frances Lincoln Limited
Text copyright © 2013 Marianne Suhr & Roger Hunt
Foreword © 2013 Kevin McCloud
Chart on page 52 © 2013 Conker Conservation Ltd
Illustrations by Libby Fellingham
Index by Marianne Ryan
Edited and designed by Jane Havell Associates Ltd

First Frances Lincoln edition published in the UK 2013

The Society for the Protection of Ancient Buildings. A charitable company limited
by guarantee. Company No. 5743962, Charity No. 111 3753, Scottish Charity
No. SC 039244

British Library cataloguing-in-publication data
A catalogue record for this book is available from the British Library

ISBN 978 0 7112 3278 5

Printed and bound in China

9 8 7 6 5 4 3

Contents

THE SOCIETY FOR THE PROTECTION
OF ANCIENT BUILDINGS

The Society for the Protection of Ancient Buildings was founded by William Morris in 1877 to counteract the highly destructive 'restoration' of medieval buildings being practised by many Victorian architects. Today it is the largest, oldest and most technically expert national pressure group fighting to save old buildings from decay, demolition and damage.

Members include many of the leading conservation practitioners as well as home owners, living in houses spanning all historical periods, and those who simply care about old buildings. Thousands of buildings survive which would have been lost, mutilated or badly repaired without the SPAB's intervention. Indeed, many of the most famous structures in Britain are cared for by some of the several thousand people who have received the Society's training.

The SPAB is a charity representing the practical and positive side of conservation, not only campaigning but educating and offering advice. Courses are run for building professionals and homeowners and information is available in the form of publications and a telephone helpline manned by experts.

A firm set of principles backed by practical knowledge, accumulated over many decades, is at the heart of the Society's approach to repair. Misguided work can be extremely destructive and the skill lies in making repairs with the minimum loss of fabric and so of beauty and authenticity – old buildings are not best preserved by 'restoring' them to make them new and perfect.

Remember, maintenance is the most practical and economic form of preservation. Buildings cannot be made to last for ever but, through the conservative approach advocated by the SPAB, they will survive as long as possible and suffer the least alteration.

More information about the Society's work and the help it can offer is available at www.spab.org.uk.

William Morris (1834–96), founder of the Society for the Protection of Ancient Buildings.

Foreword

There are some 26 million homes in Britain, most of them as well insulated as a rabbit hutch, most of which will still be in existence in 2050. Half a million of them are listed; countless numbers sit in conservation areas and, very roughly, one fifth of our dwellings were built before 1919.

Collectively, the buildings we live in are responsible for more or less 26 per cent of Britain's carbon emissions. Now, you may be among the dwindling number of people who believe that increased levels of atmospheric carbon dioxide have got nothing to do with human activity and that we can do nothing about that. You may cry humbug to the Greens among us and eschew words such as sustainability and eco as mere baubles of conversational fashion. But I doubt that, because you've already picked this book up.

In any case, it doesn't require a lifetime membership of Greenpeace to appreciate that the planet's resources are finite, that the world population is growing beyond sustainable levels and that our homes gobble energy to keep us warm and fed. Generally speaking, the older and larger our homes are, the more energy they consume. Any owner of an historic home will be sensitised to the cost of this and to the volatility of energy markets just by reading their electricity, gas or oil bills. Indeed, some of the nation's more august historic homeowners have responded over the past ten years by investing in low-carbon and independent technologies such as solar photovoltaic and biomass boilers to reduce the sheer cost of heating and maintaining their properties.

The rest of us shiver at the capital cost of a wood-pellet boiler with auger-feed and ash-compacter and just don another pullover. So three green cheers for this book, which mixes an erudite analysis of the latest building science with practical advice and demonstrations of best practice. It behoves any proud carer of an old home to arm themselves with an outline understanding of dewpoints, interstitial condensation and U-values, and – do not fret, dear Reader – these are all admirably and sometimes even entertainingly explained and illustrated here. More hurrahs! Moreover, they are helpfully framed in the context of what is good conservation practice, of the need for reversibility and for the retention of our buildings' narratives. These ideas are part of the bedrock of The Society for the Protection of Ancient Buildings, this book's co-publisher.

Britain's older housing is immensely varied, dependent on vernacular styles and a vast range of materials that give the historic built environment of the British Isles a great deal of charm and diversity. We can't just slap insulation board over every home in the country and then apply a coat of efficient German render. Our older homes need a delicate touch and tailored solutions that will involve professional architects and historic building surveyors but which ultimately will rely upon the informed enthusiasm of homeowners.

This book treads the brave and narrow path between the slippery pitfalls of the eco agenda on the one hand and the treacherous skewers of conservation on the other. Green building and traditional building may seem likely bedfellows – they share a love of natural, breathing materials such as lime mortar and doglick; but this common interest is a narrow one and in truth there is a great deal of compromise to be forged, between their separate demands, on any building conservation project. This book is intended, lucidly and comfortably, to guide you along that path.

KEVIN McCLOUD

Kevin McCloud, author, broadcaster and designer.

ADVISORY NOTE

Please note that the information given here is based on the best current practice. But every building is different, and so specific recommendations or suggestions may not necessarily be relevant in every instance. They should not be applied automatically. If you are in any doubt, do seek suitably experienced professional advice. This also relates to the photographs and illustrations which indicate an approach, but which should not be treated as a guarantee of the correct method in every set of circumstances. Site safety and building methods shown in the photographs are not necessarily best practice or endorsed by the authors or the SPAB.

Retrofitting old buildings is a new and constantly evolving science. Generally, natural and breathable products are favoured but as every situation is different the consequences of any intervention cannot be predicted with certainty. Before applying any method, material or detail, always seek the advice of the manufacturer or supplier or check with a qualified professional as to whether or not it is appropriate to your particular building.

Research is a vital part of any work to an old building. The SPAB website, bookshop and technical advice line are geared towards helping homeowners, craftspeople and professional advisers and can provide the latest information. For this reason, lists of organisations, suppliers and publications that might quickly date have not been included here.

Historic environment consents

Given the vast number of different areas of work covered in this book, it would be difficult, if not repetitive, to draw attention to all the circumstances in which consent may be required to make changes. This omission does not mean that the matter should be disregarded. Quite the contrary; the UK has strict laws which protect historic buildings, areas, sites and landscapes and it is in your interest to adhere to these.

Before beginning any work of repair, alteration or development to your house, any structures within its grounds or the site on which it stands, it is essential to check with your local planning authority whether any consent will be needed. In the case of all listed buildings, do remember that the interior as well as the exterior is protected, and that the listing may extend to ancillary structures within the main building's curtilage (the land attached to it). When consent is granted, work must follow the approved drawings exactly, as well as any conditions that have been imposed.

Preface

When we wrote *Old House Handbook*, thoughts of energy-efficiency and carbon reduction in relation to old houses were only just emerging into mainstream consciousness. How times have changed. Now 'eco-retrofitting' buildings to make them more energy-efficient and sustainable is seen as an integral part of repair and maintenance. But in the rush to be 'eco', compatibility between traditional buildings and modern technologies can easily be ignored. This is potentially a huge mistake, with far-reaching consequences. The knock-on effects must be considered in relation to every-thing, from improved airtightness and thermal insulation to the installation of solar panels. If not carefully thought through, these potentially irreversible changes could jeopardise the future of our built heritage.

We have sought to offer a holistic approach to improving the energy-efficiency, comfort and sustain-ability of solid-walled traditional structures. While this book stands on its own, the basics of repairing an old house are laid down in *Old House Handbook* so the two books should be regarded as companion volumes. The retrofitting of old buildings is a comparatively young science – there is disagreement about some methods and materials, even among experts in the field.

Everyone who takes on an old building has different levels of knowledge and ability, so we have not set out to give detailed step-by-step guidance. Neither have we attempted to explain the workings of technology, as this information is widely available elsewhere. What we hope to share with you is practical advice and the desire to do the right thing for old buildings, for the wider envi-ronment and for the future.

MARIANNE SUHR
ROGER HUNT

Old houses can be green

William Morris, founder of the SPAB, said: 'We are only trustees for those that come after us.' He was referring to buildings, but today this statement could equally apply to the wider environment. Our challenge is to balance the need to be sustainable with the care of our built heritage, without destroying what is important.

Whether it is a medieval timber-framed house, an Edwardian brick terrace or any period, style or material in between, old houses are special. Bringing them up to modern-day energy-efficiency levels is not about quick fixes. Many fall into the 'hard to treat' category, most commonly because they have walls of traditional construction that are often solid. These are difficult to insulate because of breathability issues, the need to retain historic fabric and the risk of ruining their appearance and character.

Numerous old buildings already possess values associated with being 'eco', 'green' and 'sustainable'. They represent an investment in natural materials. Importantly, they are a valuable resource for the future – especially when successfully retrofitted to improve their energy-efficiency and reduce their environmental impact – and have a significant role to play in maintaining communities with character and aesthetic interest. Old houses frequently have high thermal mass, helping to prevent overheating in summer; use natural materials in their construction, and have components which are easy to repair. The materials used to build them are generally reusable.

Opposite: Just like classic cars, old houses need to be treated sympathetically; retrofitting may not always be appropriate.

Right: Improving a building's thermal efficiency is important, but we must take care not to create problems for the future.

There is no doubt that we must reduce carbon dioxide (CO_2) emissions from buildings, but we must take care in the process. Without fully understanding how a building works there is a very real risk that, at some point in the future, we may find ourselves rectifying problems created by the use of ill judged techniques and materials.

WHAT IS SUSTAINABILITY?

We cannot think about cutting carbon emissions in buildings in isolation: we must consider sustainability in its broader sense. Sustainability concerns dwindling resources. To use the key statement on sustainable development coined by the Brundtland Commission in 1987, it is about 'development that meets the needs of the present without compromising the ability of future generations to meet their own needs'.

To live sustainably is to tread lightly on the earth. It means living within our means in terms of resources; minimising pollution to the air, soil and water, and respecting the wider environment of animals, birds, insects, plants and trees. Scrutinising the life cycle of products, eliminating carbon emissions from intensive energy use and reducing our dependence on fossil fuels are all part of this, as is creating strong communities and pleasant places to live.

UNDERSTANDING OLD BUILDINGS

Old buildings have a subtle, intangible, hard-to-define quality or character. This is related to texture, irregularity and the patina of age – it may be seen in a brick floor worn by centuries of use, gently undulating plasterwork or a lopsided window resulting from the slight settlement of a wall. Once disfigured or destroyed, such subtleties can never be reinstated and their aesthetic and historic value is lost forever. Equally, the materials and techniques used in the construction of old buildings are special and have qualities not found in the mass-produced materials of today.

When damage occurs, it is frequently more through ignorance than deliberate intent. Many people see themselves as the guardians rather than the owners of old buildings and, by carefully balancing the needs of today with those of the past, help ensure their houses have a viable future. The golden rule is to do as little as possible and no more than is necessary.

Above: The special qualities of an old building, such as those seen in this village house, can be easily destroyed if they are not appreciated.

Right: This sash window has been carefully repaired, and the rotten cill replaced.

Opposite: The early twentieth century saw the final flourish of traditional building techniques.

Repair not restore

Caring for old buildings is about preventing any unnecessary loss to the building's fabric. The general approach to building conservation was established in 1877 when William Morris founded The Society for the Protection of Ancient Buildings (SPAB). In its manifesto he set out a philosophy of repair rather than restoration which guides the Society's work to this day.

Repair is based on the principle of mending buildings with the minimum loss of fabric and in so doing keeping their character and authenticity. Contrary to this, restoration means work intended to return an old building to a perfect state. In other words, putting things back to how they were, or how we think they were, rather than preserving them as they are now with all their wonderful scars of time and history. Restoration is generally highly destructive and, as Morris states in the manifesto, 'a feeble and lifeless forgery is the final result of all the wasted labour'.

Putting the philosophy outlined by Morris into practice means, for example, repairing only the decayed bottom rail of an original sash window rather than replacing the whole sash. The aim is not to hide imperfections such as bulges, bows, sags and leans but rather to respect and enjoy them. Remember that an approach that involves SPAB-minded conservative repair is likely to be the least costly, the 'greenest' and the most enduring; and it will probably maximise the value of your house in the longer term.

ESSENTIAL DIFFERENCES

The building techniques that we know today began to be introduced in the second half of the nineteenth century, with cement-based mortars, renders and plasters coming into general use by the late 1940s. These techniques rely on impervious outer layers, cavity walls and barriers against moisture – systems which are totally incompatible with traditional solid-wall construction which works in a very different way. In addition, there has been a propensity for creating 'hermetically' sealed interiors with central heating and little air movement – this, if not correctly managed, will be at odds with the way an older building works. Cavity walls, though occasionally used by the Victorians, became popular in the early twentieth century and have since been adopted as a standard method of construction.

Until that time, most buildings had solid walls, and this older form accounts for an estimated one out of every five homes in the UK. In solid-walled, traditionally built buildings, the bricks and stones were generally bonded with weak and porous mortars made of lime and sand, sometimes just earth or clay. When external walls constructed with these materials – and others such as 'cob' (earth) – were rendered, lime render was used and this was often limewashed. This means the structure was able to 'breathe'. When it rained, moisture was absorbed a few millimetres into the external surface but was able to evaporate when the rain stopped, helped by the drying effects of the sun and wind.

Inside, walls were plastered with lime or even clay and finished with simple breathable paints such as limewash. Any excess internal humidity from laundry, cooking and human activity was dispersed by way of open flues and draughts, or absorbed by the breathable surfaces that acted as moisture buffers. In addition, a kitchen range and open fires drew air through the house and kept internal surfaces at a steady temperature. Provided such buildings are properly maintained, the structures remain essentially dry and in equilibrium.

In recent times, the understanding of how traditional solid walls work has become confused, and builders have tried to apply modern techniques and impermeable materials to breathing structures. Cement renders, along with 'plastic' paints, waterproof sealants, damp-proof membranes and even insulation materials can act as barriers to the building's natural ability to breathe. This is where the trouble occurs: the new technologies trap water within permeable materials and exacerbate the very problems that they are trying to resolve. Consequently, buildings become damp, unhealthy and less thermally efficient. Since wet walls

are less thermally efficient than dry ones, maintenance is essential. Inappropriate alterations are also likely to lead to major works and repairs to the fabric in years to come, resulting in waste, further costs and the use of yet more materials and resources.

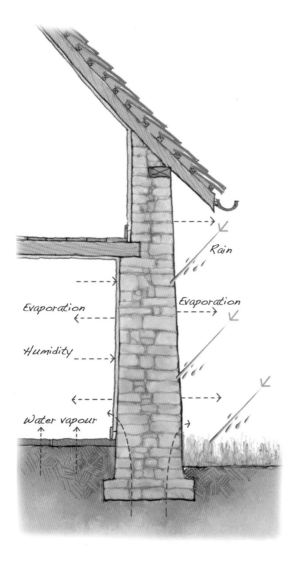

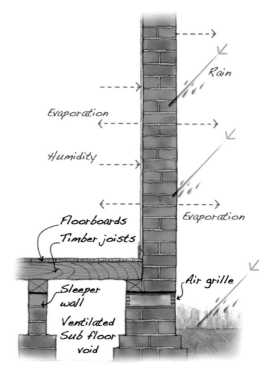

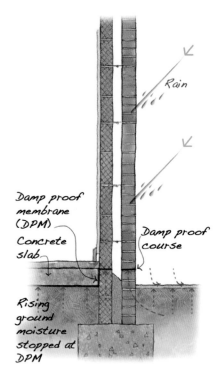

Traditional solid walls were built and plastered in breathable lime and clay mixes. They absorbed and released moisture, and readily evaporated rising damp.

From the mid-nineteenth century, brick buildings often incorporated suspended timber floors and slate damp-proof courses but remained breathable, solid-walled structures.

Modern cavity walls work on an entirely different principle from the breathing wall: they are designed to block moisture transfer at every junction and every surface.

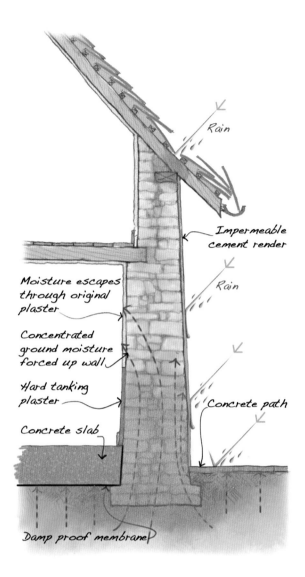

Rain

Impermeable
cement render

Moisture escapes
through original
plaster

Rain

Concentrated
ground moisture
forced up wall

Hard tanking
plaster

Concrete path

Concrete slab

Damp proof membrane

Breathing, solid walls are not generally compatible with impermeable modern materials. By applying cement renders, concrete floor slabs and plastic membranes, moisture can become trapped, resulting in dampness, timber decay and a thermally inefficient wall.

LIME

The use of lime products is essential to the wellbeing of old buildings. Unlike cement-based materials they produce soft textures, offer flexibility and, most important of all, are permeable so allow walls to breathe and shed moisture, thus avoiding damp. As lime dries out it carbonates and absorbs CO_2.

Lime is made from any naturally occurring calcium carbonate such as limestone, chalks or even seashells which are burnt in a kiln to form quicklime. There are two basic types of lime: non-hydraulic and hydraulic. Non-hydraulic lime is produced from pure limestone and comes in the form of 'lime putty' which offers the greatest flexibility and breathability of all the limes. Nataural hydraulic limes are produced from limestones with naturally occurring impurities, primarily clay. These produce limes that set quicker and harder; supplied in dry powder form, they start to set when they come into contact with water. While suitable for some applications, they do not offer the same degree of breathability as non-hydraulic lime. A third type of lime is often referred to as hydrated or 'bagged' lime: this is fundamentally a powdered form of non-hydraulic lime putty but is not generally recommended as a substitute.

Choosing the right lime products is key but should not be daunting. Using ready-mixed lime mortars and limewashes makes life easy and lime suppliers are generally happy to offer advice. There are a variety of courses available and it is well worth encouraging your builders to have training, or to get an on-site trainer, if they are unfamiliar with using lime.

Right: Calcium carbonate, here in the form of limestone, forms the basis of all lime building products.

Right: Lime is slaked to produce lime putty.

Using lime

Natural hydraulic lime comes in a variety of strengths, with the prefix NHL (natural hydraulic lime) and a number (e.g. NHL 2, NHL 3.5 or NHL 5) to denote the proportion of clay and other impurities contained within the original limestone. These impurities act as setting agents and the higher the number the less flexible and breathable the mortar or plaster will be. This means that a suitable type of lime can be specified for any situation, even in exposed or damp conditions, or where it needs to set quickly or be particularly strong.

As with any material, health and safety issues should be considered. Lime is particularly caustic and can cause damage if splashed in your eyes, so wear goggles and gloves. When dealing with it in powdered form, wear a mask. Having eye wash close at hand is essential and always wash your hands after using lime-based materials.

Right: The putty is matured before being mixed with sand to form mortars, plasters and renders.

Far right: Hydraulic lime mortar is used here to lay new bricks.

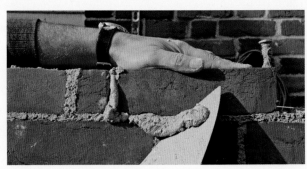

THE NEED FOR CARE

The enduring appeal of old buildings is testament to how they were built and the quality and nature of the materials used. Their layout, the size of rooms and the way they were constructed potentially makes them highly adaptable to modern life. Indeed, single Georgian and Victorian houses are often successfully converted into a number of smaller units to meet changing demand and the trend towards smaller households.

This helps make older buildings more sustainable but remember, in attempting to turn an old building into an eco building a point may be reached where conservation principles and good practice are compromised to such an extent that the building loses its historic relevance and character. You may be in danger of destroying the very things which originally attracted you to it and made it special.

NATURAL EQUILIBRIUM

Vernacular architecture grew from its location. For many traditional buildings, materials were gathered locally from the surrounding countryside. This contributed to the distinctiveness of our regions and the vernacular styles of our towns and villages. By definition most of these materials were natural: timber, clay, stone, thatch. Even when the transportation of goods from one place to another was made easier by the canals and later the railways, the materials used remained predominantly natural in their origins. The difference was that they were mass-produced rather than handmade.

Repairable

The handmade nature of many of the building components used in the past means that they are easily repaired should they fail, so fewer natural resources are used. The most obvious examples are timber windows and doors. It is relatively easy for a good carpenter to cut out a broken or rotten section, such as the bottom rail of a sash window, and insert a replacement part. The same is generally not true with modern products, such as those made of PVCu, where it is frequently necessary to replace the entire unit, even if the damage is fairly minor.

Top: Unsympathetic replacement windows and modern masonry paint have destroyed the character of this quaint Victorian row.

Above left: Vernacular buildings used local materials and traditions and were a response to their particular site.

Left: 'Repairability' is a key aspect of being green.

Above: These old bricks have been cleaned up and reused.

Architectural salvage

While recycling building materials is sometimes a good thing, it is important to remember that the provenance of second-hand items should always be verified to avoid architectural theft or vandalism. Many roofs have been stripped of their tiles and fireplaces ripped out simply for monetary gain, leaving the building they formed a part of open to the elements and devoid of history and character.

Right: Always check the provenance of items such as fireplaces.

Recyclable and reusable

From palaces to humble cottages, many buildings have been constructed of material recycled from earlier structures. The beauty of traditional materials is that they can often be reused, sometimes extending the life of buildings by many hundreds of years.

Walling components bonded together with lime mortar and covered with lime renders and plasters are often salvageable. While lime mortar works well when holding bricks together in compression, it is relatively easily cleaned off the surface of a brick when a wall is deconstructed. Consequently a brick that has been bonded, rendered or plastered with lime is easily recycled into a new wall. A brick bonded with cement-based mortar is far less likely to be reused as it is almost impossible to remove the mortar.

Other traditional building materials such as cob and daub may be reconstituted for use in repairs so there is little or no waste. Timber can be reused for other purposes and, at the end of its life, be burnt for heat. Materials such as thatch are biodegradable so suitable for composting.

Similarly, care should be taken not to confuse the history of a building by introducing materials such as old beams from elsewhere in situations where new equivalents are available. Indeed, it is often preferable to use traditional materials made new rather than those that have been salvaged because maintaining their long-term availability may be more sustainable than the cannibalistic chase of an ever-decreasing supply.

Remember that some reused materials might be nearing the end of their life. For example, clay roof tiles can fail soon after being reused because of inherent frost damage, while salvaged bricks may have been in chimneys where flue gases have reduced their effectiveness. Some bricks may be unsuitable for outside walls as they were originally of poor quality and deliberately placed where they were not at risk of weather, perhaps in party walls.

Left: Flooring is commonly resold in architectural salvage yards.

ENERGY PERFORMANCE

Until comparatively recently, little attention was paid to the energy performance of buildings. Now running costs and energy use are prime considerations and a key factor in a building's ongoing sustainability.

Measuring performance

Setting aside the goals of reducing CO_2 emissions and cutting fuel bills, there is another reason to think about making a building 'green': in the future, green properties are likely to have extra value and be more highly sought after.

The energy-efficiency of homes can be measured in various ways. The most relevant when you buy, rent or sell a property are Energy Performance Certificates (EPCs). These show the building's performance in bands similar to those used to indicate the efficiency of electrical appliances. In the longer term, EPCs could result in energy-inefficient buildings becoming less desirable and more difficult to sell or rent. Conversely, EPCs could be used as a tool to force building owners to undertake work and efficiency measures that are unnecessary, poorly considered or excessive.

EPCs are undertaken by qualified assessors, regulated by an approved accreditation scheme, who visit the building and input data about features such as boilers, heating controls, insulation and windows into a computer programme called RdSAP or Reduced Data SAP (Standard Assessment Procedure). It is this that calculates the energy-efficiency of the building and its environmental impact; recommendations are then made for improving energy-efficiency.

The EPC is an asset rating, and models the energy consumption of the property on the basis of standard occupancy, making assumptions about the number of people living there, the demand temperature for the heating system and the heating pattern. Consequently, the EPC does not always reflect the actual energy consumption of the property. It is also limited in the sense that the recommendations generated are very broad and do not take into account specific issues relating to the property such as planning requirements, conservation issues and the structural suitability of the house for certain measures.

Unfortunately, the information and recommendations provided by EPCs may result in owners being persuaded to 'upgrade' buildings in an attempt to improve their performance by using methods which are damaging to their fabric and spoil what makes them special. And the money this work may cost does not always equate with the payback of the measures being taken. More worrying still, inappropriate measures may have to be removed and remedial work undertaken in the future, which is not only expensive and wasteful but completely unsustainable.

Above: This Grade I listed building features precious pargetting. Worryingly, however, among the recommendations, the EPC lists external wall insulation.

Top: Energy use and carbon emissions are factors at every stage of a building's life from construction to demolition.

Above: These boarded-up houses in Nelson, Lancashire, are under threat of demolition.

Embodied energy and carbon

Improving the buildings we live in today often makes a lot more sense than pulling them down and starting again by building new structures. Indeed, it is sometimes argued that an existing building is more sustainable than one built tomorrow, especially if its performance in terms of energy use can be improved.

This has to do with the energy required to erect a building and operate it. Energy used for the erection of a building is called embodied energy; that used in the operation of a building is called operational energy. Generating energy for these activities often results in emissions of carbon dioxide – for example, when energy is produced by burning fossil fuels, such as coal, gas or oil. Therefore, embodied energy has embodied carbon dioxide emissions (embodied carbon) associated with it, and operational energy goes alongside operational carbon.

There are no universally accepted definitions of either embodied energy or embodied carbon. Broadly, for a building, embodied energy refers to the quantity of energy, expressed in kWh or kJ, related to its construction. This includes the energy expended in raw material extraction, the manufacture of building products and construction on site, as well as any energy used to transport those materials and products. Embodied carbon, measured in kg, is the amount of carbon emitted by these processes.

Therefore retaining an existing building, instead of replacing it with a new one, means that the embodied energy and carbon required to construct a new building are avoided. A new replacement building would need to be much more energy-efficient than the old one; in other words, have a significantly lower operational energy. It must also be long-lasting in order to recover over time the amount of energy required for, and the amount of carbon emitted from, its erection – its embodied energy.

An important distinction exists between embodied energy and carbon. The amount of embodied energy used for the construction of a house remains the same no matter what the source of energy employed. The quantity of embodied carbon will depend entirely on the means of generating that energy. For example, if a brick is fired using energy generated by wind or hydro power, or it is unfired and baked in the sun, there will be little or no carbon emitted during its production. If the energy generated is from fossil fuels such as coal, gas or oil, the level of carbon is likely to be high. Naturally this concept extends to the energy used at all other stages of the process, from the extraction of the raw materials to transportation to site. For example, timber extracted from woodland using horses has far lower embodied energy and carbon than if mechanical means have been used.

Given all these factors, defining and comparing energy and carbon emissions are far from straightforward. The various methodologies and data used, and the difficulties that result, can give a wide range of embodied values for any given material or process.

Orientation

From north-lit artists' studios to nineteenth-century 'butterfly plan' houses, people have understood the importance of orientation in buildings. In the context of sustainability, orientation is as important as ever and worth remembering when buying and planning a house because it is a factor in helping to cut energy costs for lighting and heating.

The light and heat from the sun are powerful allies and frustrating foes. They can reduce the energy requirement of a building but may cause overheating and fade fabrics and works of art. Equally, the direction of the prevailing wind and rain might make a difference to the way a house works and the range of problems encountered with damp and cold.

Thermal mass

Many old buildings have good thermal mass. Thermal mass, or 'thermal capacity' in the most general sense, describes the ability of any material to absorb, store and then release heat over time. Heavyweight construction materials such as brick and stone act rather like storage heaters, absorbing and releasing heat, so can help moderate temperature fluctuations to create a comfortable and largely self-regulating internal living environment.

When used appropriately, the stabilising or 'buffering' effect of thermal mass helps prevent overheating during the summer and reduces the need for mechanical cooling. Similarly, the ability to store heat can help reduce fuel usage by capturing, and later releasing, solar gains and heat from internal appliances. Thermal mass is particularly useful for buildings in more southerly latitudes where there are large temperature

Above: This artist's studio was built in the early twentieth century, with a north-facing double-height window to exploit natural light.

swings between day and night. This is likely to become important in the future if temperatures become more extreme due to climate change.

Thermal mass is not a substitute for insulation but the two do have a bearing on one another and can influence decisions as to how and whether to insulate. If insulation is fitted internally, it separates the heated interior from the mass of exterior heavyweight walls which then no longer provide heat storage. There will still be gains from heavy internal walls and solid floors which will store and release heat.

The disadvantage with thermal mass is that it is comparatively slow to work. Houses with dense masonry walls take much longer and use more energy to heat up than those built with well insulated lightweight materials.

Above: Buildings with thick stone walls benefit from high thermal mass, helping to regulate internal temperature.

ENJOYMENT

Appreciating the eco credentials of your building is hugely valuable. Equally it is important not to let them overtake your enjoyment of what you have. Before rushing in to make changes, live with the building, ideally through all seasons, to understand how it reacts to changing climatic conditions. Keep an accurate record of your energy consumption, including gas and electricity readings and even the quantity of logs or other fuels that are consumed. This will give you a benchmark to work from. Everything you do in relation to greening your old building should be aimed at reducing that consumption.

During the year, monitor any obvious areas of heat loss and analyse how you use the internal spaces. You will gain a greater understanding of how the building works, enabling you to make better informed decisions for the future. This process should allow your ideas to evolve and will help you see where efficiencies can be made so that you can create a sustainable and happy place to live.

Below: Where justified, careful and considered intervention is the best way of sustaining an old building's interest.

Old house to eco house

The task of 'retrofitting' any old building to be more energy-efficient and sustainable needs careful thought right from the start. A holistic approach is vital since no single element will create an eco building and some may conflict: it is about balancing the particular needs of a traditional structure with environmental concerns.

There is a real danger that ill-thought-through retrofitting of old buildings will destroy the very things that make them sought after, comfortable and healthy and therefore inherently sustainable. Making poor choices now will be damaging, costly and wasteful of resources in the future if remedial work has to be undertaken.

The first consideration is how energy use and CO_2 emissions can be cut by reducing the need for heating. This 'fabric first' approach often involves relatively simple measures, such as installing appropriate insulation, and it should happen before you look at ways of generating energy. Adopting a long-term, holistic approach is essential as this will minimise damage to the building, save you money, prevent waste and create the most appropriate and enduring solution.

There is no standard formula to suit every house. How you proceed will depend on the constraints of the individual building; whether you are undertaking a total refurbishment or working room by room; what else you are proposing to do; if listed building and other consents are required and, importantly, your budget.

With every measure, consider the payback, both in terms of the time it takes to recoup the money spent

Opposite: Terraces like this can easily be spoilt if an individual house is unsympathetically retrofitted.

Above: Some retrofit measures have a greater visual impact than others.

through reduced energy bills and the carbon saved. It is not always the most obvious, expensive or complicated measures that produce the greatest savings. Above all, think how anything you do may affect the history, character and workings of the building.

FUTURE PROOFING

Always try to do everything possible to increase the energy-efficiency and comfort levels in your house when the opportunity arises. The last thing you want is to have to revisit work you have already done; upgrades in the future will be difficult, more costly and wasteful of resources and are likely to cause harm to the building's historic fabric. This is especially true in the case of major renovations or extensions when the work is unlikely to be revisited for many decades. For instance, if you are

retiling the roof, take the opportunity to insulate it from above.

Give yourself time, carefully research what is available and invest in the fabric of the building. Where funds are limited look for options that allow more eco-friendly additions in the future. For example, if installing a new boiler or hot water cylinder, choose one that will allow a solar thermal system to be fitted at a later date.

Bear in mind that many new technologies are likely to be superseded relatively quickly so they should be installed in ways that allow them to be removed with minimum damage to the building. Adding or renewing plumbing and wiring is particularly damaging to the fabric of old buildings so, wherever possible, provide access hatches and try to think ahead so that changes can be made easily in the future. This is especially true in bathroom and kitchen areas that tend to be refurbished frequently (➠ Cable ducting, page 164).

Left: Thinking through work at an early stage is important to avoid unnecessary damage to the building and a waste of resources.

Below: In theory, it takes 97.6 years before the cost of replacement double-glazed windows is recouped.

PAYBACK

The time it takes to recoup your investment in energy-generation and efficiency measures through the savings you make on your fuel and other bills is known as the payback period. In theory, this is an easy calculation achieved by dividing the capital cost of the improvement by the estimated annual saving.

In practice, it is not always that simple. The wide range of options available differ greatly in price and effectiveness. Costs and payback periods will vary from house to house and depend on the exact specification of the measures being proposed. Payback time includes the cost of installation and fees for consultants. In addition, any available grants, subsidies or loans must be considered.

As well as the financial costs, thought should be given to how much each measure is likely to reduce CO_2 emissions over its life. This is not all: the energy payback of a system has to be considered. For example, how long will a solar panel have to operate to recover the energy used to manufacture it in the first place? Equally, the amount of embodied energy and carbon used to source, manufacture and transport the materials and components should be borne in mind. It is worth remembering that in some cases the warranty on products is shorter than the potential payback time so replacement may be necessary before payback has been achieved.

Some of the figures for payback times based on a three-bedroom semi-detached house are surprising. For example, loft insulation has an estimated 2.7-year payback while the potential carbon savings are 190kg per year. If installing windows with double glazing, in theory it will take 97.6 years to get your money back and will result in a carbon saving of just 26 kg per year. In practice, many homeowners report double-glazed units lasting less than twenty years.

A worrying paradox is that increased energy-efficiency tends to lead us to consume more energy. This hypothesis has been dubbed the Khazzoom-Brookes postulate. Our behaviour is therefore a crucial factor in cutting emissions and saving energy; it is vital that all measures introduced are easy to use and new technology is not so baffling that it is used inefficiently.

Aside from these financial and environmental aspects, it is worth remembering the wider benefits energy-efficiency measures offer in terms of comfort and wellbeing. A home that is hard to heat can be unsustainable because it is uncomfortable and damp so may cause health problems and result in the need for added maintenance.

Above: Every old house is different, and requires a bespoke solution when considering retrofitting.

Minor work, major benefits

Before embarking on retrofit projects, think about doing simple things that do not cost much but often provide worthwhile savings and increase comfort:

> Insulate roof spaces and pipes.
> Draughtproof doors, windows and floorboards.
> Deal with the source of damp problems.
> Carry out regular maintenance.
> Close curtains and shutters just before it gets dark to keep in the heat of the day and stop draughts.
> Buy an energy monitor to understand your energy use.
> Review the timings on your heating controls.
> Turn down the thermostat by a couple of degrees and overhaul the heating system.
> Heat the rooms you use, not the whole house.
> Replace old light bulbs with low-energy lamps.
> Install 'A'-rated appliances and turn them off when not in use.
> Dress appropriately – wear warmer clothes!

Above: An energy monitor is a first step towards understanding your usage.

HOLISTIC APPROACH

Retrofitting poses more than tricky technical questions. It has the potential to raise issues associated with the aesthetics and history of the building, its structure and the way it was originally designed to keep damp at bay. Importantly, no two properties are the same: materials, location, design and orientation vary. Detached houses with a large exposed external area benefit most from improved thermal efficiency; smaller attached buildings tend to gain more from the introduction of renewable energy.

The key is to make an old house energy-efficient without destroying its integrity, or compromising the way it functions. It is vital to look at the whole building, to take a holistic approach and to understand that each thing you do may potentially have both a positive and negative impact.

The right time

When considering the installation of technology, remember that this is constantly developing and may in future reduce in size and weight. Where such innovations are likely to result in less damage being done to the building, it may be worth deferring the installation of these systems. The same applies to energy-efficiency measures such as internal wall insulation where its true impact on the fabric of buildings is not yet known.

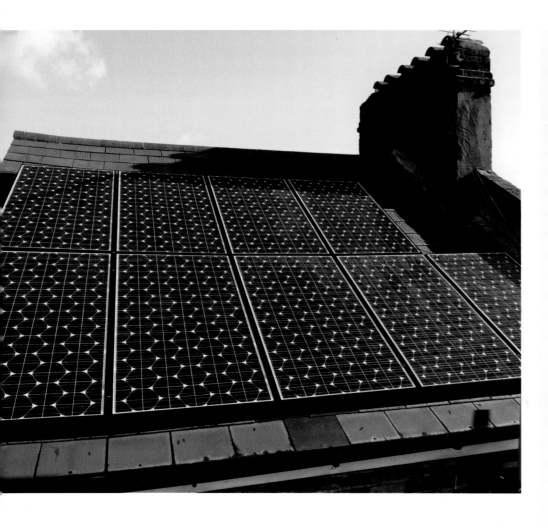

Above: Technology such as these photovoltaic panels is ever-changing so it is worth thinking carefully about the most appropriate solutions.

Holistic steps

There are three steps towards making a house more energy-efficient and sustainable. These should always be based on a holistic approach with a master plan that focuses on how all the various measures will ultimately work effectively together.

> Quick wins: simple and easily reversible DIY measures that are achievable, affordable, cause the minimum disruption and potentially offer significant immediate gains. These include draughtproofing, fitting low-energy lightbulbs, installing loft insulation and overhauling the heating system.

> Exploiting opportunities: there are numerous examples of upgrades that can be undertaken when other work is done. If a new boiler is required, choose a model with the highest energy performance but also consider whether it will work with other technologies in the future, such as a solar thermal system. Where windows need repair or replacement, look at the options for draughtproofing and secondary glazing.

> Major renovation: this allows significant opportunities for everything from wall insulation to grey water recycling and heat pumps.

Left: Concentrate on the quick wins such as loft insulation, in this case using sheep's wool, before considering more invasive measures.

MAINTENANCE

Maintenance is the most important single thing to consider when caring for any building. It has huge benefits because it saves wasteful replacement and the use of new materials while resulting in increased thermal efficiency, comfort, cash savings and a reduction in CO_2 emissions. For example:

> Promptly replacing a missing slate or tile saves damage to timber rafters and plaster ceilings due to damp and rot.

> Clearing out or repairing gutters and downpipes means walls stay dry: wet walls are less thermally efficient than dry ones.

> Replacing defective pointing has similar benefits but only if lime mortar is used. Traditional lime mortar is necessary because it is a breathable, flexible mortar that contains no cement.

> Fixing a broken pane of glass or making sure a window fits snugly keeps heat in and stops draughts.

> Replacing a tap washer will prevent water wastage and save the use of chemicals to remove water stains from sanitary ware.

Top: Lack of maintenance accelerates decay in old houses.

Above: A thermal imaging camera is a useful way of learning more about your house.

BE PROPERLY INFORMED

Buildings are often unwittingly damaged through lack of knowledge. Understanding your home, its materials, structure, history and surroundings should be a priority and often proves to be much of the fun of ownership. Books and magazines are useful resources and the web is invaluable – but beware, there is a vast amount of misinformation, confusion and conflicting opinions, so do your research thoroughly. 'Green' and 'eco' are words readily bandied around so it is important not to be misled by 'greenwash' and unfounded claims, particularly of breathability. Always try to seek out impartial advice and be wary of those offering help who have something to sell.

Thinking about the skills and materials you may need early on could save you money. When it comes to employing professionals, it will help give you a clearer idea of whether they have a feel for the needs of the building and understand sustainable principles.

With old buildings it is not always possible to know the extent of the undertaking until you begin. Often they hold secrets; records of past work, even where they exist, can be inaccurate or misleading. The work may also be considerably more expensive because of the need to source and use traditional materials and craftspeople, so never underestimate the cost of completing the project. Work out what you can afford and, if you go ahead, prioritise the work. Always allow a contingency in terms of both time and cost.

Advice

The SPAB supplies advice over the telephone as well as details of specialist craftspeople and building professionals. It runs courses and events to provide homeowners with the knowledge necessary to make informed decisions about the repair of buildings and has a range of publications which are highly respected for giving authoritative and practical guidance.

Above: Plan the interior layout to exploit natural light.

Right: Before undertaking major works, ensure you have the necessary consents in place.

PLANNING THE INTERIOR

Good interior design is about more than just using sustainable products and materials, it takes account of emotions and influences wellbeing. It embraces everything from light, colour, materials and textures to layout, ergonomics and acoustics. The way tactile elements and spaces are brought together, the flow of the rooms, the orientation of the building and the introduction of sunlight all contribute to the energy-efficiency and sustainability of an old building.

When thinking about a building's interior, bear in mind that living spaces generally have higher requirements for daylight. The use of natural daylight is beneficial to health and minimises the need for artificial light so should be maximised for work areas such as kitchens and home offices. Bathrooms and bedrooms need far less natural light so are best located on the north side of a building. Similarly, natural ventilation results in less dependence on mechanical ventilation.

Durability is essential to sustainable design. If items are inherently fragile, poorly made or difficult to maintain, they will be quickly replaced at further environmental cost.

Importantly, interior design needs to make sustainable behaviour within a household easy. For example, designated places for drying clothes and storing recyclable waste are useful, while energy monitors displayed in a prominent position help you understand energy use.

Practical measures such as fitting doors in corridors and circulation spaces will reduce air movement in draughty interiors, although they must be designed so they can be left open during warmer months to aid ventilation. Similarly, fitting a curtain at the bottom of a staircase can help cut draughts caused by warm air rising.

RULES AND REGULATIONS

Consent from the local planning authority may be required when carrying out work to listed buildings, buildings within conservation areas, scheduled ancient monuments and buildings which are of architectural and historical interest within national parks and areas of outstanding natural beauty. In addition, planning permission and building regulation approval may be needed.

A listed building is protected in its entirety, inside and out, regardless of the listing grade, and structures within its 'curtilage' – the land around it – can be covered in the listing too. This may mean that there will be limitations on internal alterations, for example the dry-lining of walls to improve thermal performance.

Invariably, most listed buildings fall into the 'hard to treat' category when it comes to energy-efficiency measures. Not only are their walls generally solid (as opposed to cavity) or framed, but their fabric is particularly sensitive, their aesthetics precious and their history profoundly important. It is unlikely that listed building consent will be granted for wall insulation applied internally or externally if it alters the character of the building.

Left: Extensions need to meet current Building Regulations.

Building Regulations

The Building Regulations are divided into parts, each relating to different aspects of construction, and are designed to ensure that buildings are safe and durable. Part L, 'Conservation of Fuel and Power', relates to energy-efficiency. Owners of old houses will be concerned with Part L1B, 'Existing Dwellings'. This refers to 'thermal elements': the walls, floors, ceilings and roofs that make up the 'thermal envelope' of the building. A garage or a conservatory is outside the thermal envelope, provided it is not heated. Part L1B also refers to 'controlled services', such as space heating, hot-water systems and fixed lighting, and 'controlled fittings' such as windows, rooflights and doors.

Existing houses do not usually have to comply with the standards set out in the Building Regulations, unless extensive work is being carried out. General repair and maintenance therefore does not have to comply with regulations.

New extensions to old buildings, however, must generally comply with the regulations set out for new buildings. The standards are reduced for 'retained thermal elements', such as existing walls, floors and roofs. L1B contains a list of target U-values (➡ page 43) relating to existing fabric which is considerably more lenient than that set out for new-build.

In simplified terms, existing buildings will need to be thermally upgraded when:

> they are subject to a 'material change of use', such as when a shop or barn is converted into a house

> there is a change in the building's 'energy status', where a building not previously subject to energy-efficiency requirements is converted into one where they do apply

> previously unheated/uninhabited spaces are converted, for example a garage or loft is converted into a habitable room

> more than 50 per cent of any thermal element is being changed or renovated. For example, more than half the wall is being re-rendered or clad, or more than half the roof covering is being stripped and re-tiled. In this instance, the whole of that thermal element would need to meet the standards

> more than 25 per cent of the total building envelope is being changed or renovated. In this instance, the whole building envelope would need to be improved
> the U-value for an existing thermal element does not meet a defined 'threshold' value

There is a conditional exemption for listed buildings, buildings within conservation areas and scheduled ancient monuments. These do not have to comply if this would unacceptably alter their character or appearance internally or externally. This means that the sash windows of a building in this category, if beyond repair and requiring replacement, could be replaced as single-glazed sashes. In addition, the Building Regulations have three extra categories that benefit from 'special considerations':

> locally listed buildings
> buildings of architectural and historic interest such as those within national parks
> buildings of traditional construction with permeable fabric that both absorbs and readily allows the evaporation of moisture

The last category recognises for the first time that solid-walled structures need to be treated differently. It goes on to say, 'When undertaking work on . . . a building that falls within one of the classes listed above, the aim should be to improve energy-efficiency as far as is reasonably practicable. The work should not prejudice the character of the host building or increase the risk of long-term deterioration of the building fabric or fittings.'

This is particularly helpful for anyone who owns an old building but does not want to be forced to install inappropriate insulation. The wording of the section makes it possible to negotiate a compatible solution within the Building Regulations.

The explanation of the Building Regulations above refers to the 2010 regulations and is by no means comprehensive. Due to the complexities involved, it is always recommended that the local building control officer is contacted to discuss the details of a project.

Top: Barn conversions require the relevant consents for change of use.

Left: Conditional exemption may help protect certain features in listed buildings and conservation areas.

Left: Try to use local
sustainable materials
wherever possible.

Below: Look for evidence of
certification when selecting
materials, such as the PEFC
label on this pack of timber.

mental impact, such as granites and marbles. Something of beauty and value tends to get passed on as part of the property rather than being ripped out and thrown into landfill.

Whole life cycle properties are important in selecting materials. We should look for materials that are gathered from sustainable sources, use less energy, preserve and protect the building where they are used, and can then be recycled and reused once the building has reached the end of its life.

Effectively these are low- or zero-carbon materials and products. They have low embodied energy – in other words, a minimum amount of energy has been required to manufacture and supply them to the point of use. They may also 'lock up' carbon, as is the case with sustainably grown renewable materials such as timber and hemp.

While this seems to be a relatively simple concept, in practice it can be hard to determine the eco credentials of a product. For example, which is going to have the lower embodied energy: a material transported across a continent but manufactured using renewable energy from hydropower, or a product produced locally but made using electricity generated by a coal-fired power station?

Forest certification schemes provide a way of defining sustainable forest management as well as third-party, independent verification that a timber source meets the definition of sustainability. The two most commonly encountered certification schemes in the UK are the Programme for the Endorsement of Forest Certification (PEFC) and the Forest Stewardship Council (FSC).

The suitability of crop-based products, such as straw for thatch and timber for many forms of structural and aesthetic purposes, is well proven over many centuries. Many products bring environmental benefit in use. These relate to better air quality, natural management of moisture levels and reductions in allergic reactions.

Crop-based materials have the potential to bring benefits relating to the environmental impact of both the production and eventual disposal of the products they comprise. These benefits are typically due to the low embodied energy of the material, reduced pollution of different types, and ease of disposal through composting.

The regulations referred to apply to England and Wales and will vary if working outside these areas. They are subject to regular amendment so, before seeking Building Regulations approval, always check which documents are current and relevant to your locality.

CHOOSING MATERIALS

When undertaking any work, think about the impact the materials will have on the environment and choose them carefully. Sadly, many manufacturers are unable or unwilling to provide data regarding their products, so it is all too easy to become mired in confusion when trying to compare products on a like-for-like basis.

Broadly, there are two ways of assessing the sustainability of materials: life cycle impacts – direct impacts from the cradle-to-grave processes involved – and sustainable sourcing. Interestingly, when it comes to life cycle impacts, this does not necessarily rule out materials that might initially appear to have a high environ-

varnishing are ideal ways to
finish this product.

FINISHED SIZE
18mmx44mm

LENGTH
2.1m

PACK QUANTITY
6

IMPORTANT
All sizes are approximate

Promoting sustainable
forest management –
For more info:
www.pefc.org
PEFC
PEFC/16-37-000

Above: Choices we make about our homes have a direct effect on our wellbeing.

WELLBEING

It is not just the fabric of old buildings that suffers from inappropriate solutions. Human health is directly affected by the built environment, both physically and psychologically. 'Sick building syndrome' is a recognised condition and may be attributed to such things as internal temperatures, light levels and, most commonly, dampness and air quality. Symptoms can include headaches, nausea, fatigue, and skin, eye, nose and throat irritation.

Studies have shown that the indoor environment can be up to ten times more polluted than the external environment, particularly worrying when we are looking for increased airtightness in buildings. Adding inappropriate thermal insulation and improving airtightness potentially can cause or exacerbate these problems, as damp and mould growth may occur. Additionally, second-hand smoke from cigarettes and 'off-gassing' from volatile organic compounds are less able to dissipate.

Radon is also an issue. Radon tests, monitoring equipment and alarms are available and should be used to determine the problem before, during and following work to improve airtightness. Where radon barriers to floors are considered necessary they may have an impact on the structure (➡ Limecrete and radon, page 128).

Contamination

Many old buildings contain materials that are potentially damaging to health, notably lead and asbestos. Until the 1960s, lead paint was commonly used, particularly on timber and metalwork, but concerns over its toxicity led to its use being banned except in some listed buildings (➡ Dealing with old lead paint, page 144). Lead water pipes are also common and you may wish to have your drinking water tested for lead content.

Left: Lead piping is common in old houses. This lead waste pipe is not a risk, but water supply pipes should be replaced.

Below: The conversion of houses into flats necessitates careful acoustic insulation in key elements such as stud walls and floors.

Asbestos was used widely in all types of buildings because of its fire resistance and thermal properties, until its harmful effects were fully realised in the mid-1980s. Asbestos may be found in boilers, heaters, pipework and materials including some textured wall finishes, roofing, floor tiles, adhesives, wall linings and doors. Asbestos fibres and dust are dangerous if inhaled. If you are unsure whether or not asbestos is present, leave well alone and consult a competent asbestos surveyor or a contractor with the proper training and equipment to deal with it.

Some buildings, especially those associated with industry, may have other sources of potential contamination such as redundant oil tanks, or may stand on or near land contaminated by chemicals or materials relating to past use. Care needs to be taken to ensure these cannot leach into water courses and cause damage to local eco systems. They may need to be dealt with by specialist contractors.

Acoustics

Refurbishment can affect the transmission of sound and is especially problematic in apartment buildings and flats. Clearly it is not possible to insulate acoustically all old buildings without destroying their special values, but insulation between floors and on walls can help. Some insulating materials are better at absorbing sound than others. For example, tongue-and-groove wood fibre-boards are particularly effective, whereas closed-cell foam boards are poor. Sound insulation between dwellings is tricky, and expert advice from an appropriately qualified person is advisable, although there are some simple points to bear in mind:

> Taking up carpets and leaving floorboards bare, or laying hard floor coverings, will create problems in rooms beneath and may change the acoustics of the room itself, so consider rugs or acoustic insulation beneath the floor.
> Fitting recessed spotlights involves cutting holes in ceilings and provides a path for noise between floors.
> Gaps around windows let in noise as well as draughts so consider draughtproofing or secondary glazing.

Below: Good communication between client, consultant and contractor is essential.

> Chimneys often allow the transmission of sound from one part of a building to another. If unused, filling the flue with insulation may prove to be the answer (➡ Chimneys, flues and fireplaces, page 155).
> Ventilation systems can be noisy and may allow the transmission of sound through ductwork.
> Avoid placing power sockets or light switches back to back as this can allow the passage of sound.

GETTING THE WORK DONE

Although retrofitting is a relatively new field, many individuals and firms purport to offer advice and services. While some are hugely knowledgeable, others are less so, and many 'specialists' and 'consultants' do not understand the special needs of older buildings. There is no easy way of finding the right person or company for your project, but doing research will help you understand the subject better and make it easier to distinguish the good from the bad.

Contractors

While old buildings have always required careful craftsmanship and attention to detail, making them energy-efficient is equally demanding. Tasks such as installing insulation and achieving airtightness require diligence if they are to be successful and unnecessary damage to the

building's fabric is to be avoided.

Even contractors who specialise in sustainable buildings may not understand older structures, so care needs to be taken to brief them carefully and to nurture a good working relationship. As with professional advisers, look for builders with a good track record and see their work. Wherever possible, get quotations from at least three contractors on a like-for-like basis, based on a proper schedule and specification prepared by a professional or consultant unless the work is very minor.

When work starts, allow time to be on site to check that it is being properly implemented. Discuss details with your contractor, and make sure this is filtering through to the tradesman or labourer executing the job. However good the reputation of the firm, remember that the quality of work will come down to the individual who is carrying it out. Always ask to see the work before it is covered up, particularly the fitting of insulation: once closed in, it is very difficult to establish whether it has been carried out to specification. Remember that jobs such as clearing roof spaces and laying new insulation can be dirty and unpleasant. If you show your appreciation to the person carrying it out, you are likely to get a better job done.

It is always wise to get the work specified and checked by an independent specialist. Never pay a contractor upfront, always in arrears.

Waste and recycling

Inevitably, building work creates waste from stripping out or demolishing existing structures. The use of new materials results in offcuts and surpluses as well as a wide range of packaging materials including cardboard boxes, timber pallets, metal banding, plastic shrink wrap, cans and bottles.

This waste is expensive to get rid of, contributes to landfill and leads to further depletion of natural resources. The SPAB philosophy of repair rather than replacement helps cut waste but it is still worth looking at further ways to reduce, reuse and recycle (➡ Recyclable and reusable, Architectural salvage, page 16).

Waste checklist

Think about how waste can be reduced.

> Choose materials that will be more easily recycled or reused in the future.

> Design new work with a view to minimising waste. For example, use standard-sized components so that unusable offcuts will be avoided.

> Try to buy materials on the understanding that any surplus can be returned.

> Oblige builders and sub-contractors to cooperate in waste minimisation as part of their contract.

> Think about ways of recycling or reusing materials.

> Wherever appropriate, recycle waste concrete and brick by using it as hardcore or in soakaways.

> Segregate waste on site to make recycling easier.

> Try to keep as much waste on site as possible to save unnecessary transport and landfill. For example, accommodate soil dug from footings in garden landscaping.

> Load skips carefully to reduce waste volume.

> Keep spares. For example, some surplus floor tiles can be stored under a kitchen unit's plinth to allow you to repair, rather than have to replace, the floor if it suffers damage.

Below: Think carefully about what goes in a skip.

Below: Using compatible materials and techniques is often the best way of making buildings sustainable.

KEEPING IT SIMPLE

The more complex a system becomes, the more opportunity there is for failure. Old buildings have lasted for hundreds of years because of their simplicity in design, and therefore their simplicity in repair. Adopt the same philosophy when retrofitting for the future by keeping the methods, systems, materials and detailing as simple as possible.

The building envelope

Ensuring the building 'envelope' – the walls, floors, roof, windows and doors – is as thermally efficient as possible is essential before thinking about 'bolt-ons' such as solar panels. Even so, great care must be taken to avoid doing anything that prevents the building's natural ability to breathe, as this may lead to damp and decay.

Solid-walled buildings work because water vapour within their structure can escape unhindered, resulting in a state of moisture equilibrium. With careful maintenance and the use of appropriate materials, these old buildings will last hundreds of years without major damp problems, but this balance is easily upset.

Consequently, upgrading and retrofitting to increase a building's thermal efficiency must be undertaken with great care. Poorly considered insulation materials and techniques may lead to moisture becoming trapped, resulting in mould and decay which is damaging to the building's fabric and the health of the occupants.

Opposite: Improving energy-efficiency sometimes comes with risks and may have unexpected consequences for your home.

Right: Even neighbouring houses have subtle differences that may affect choices made about retrofitting.

Every building is different: there is no one-size-fits-all solution and the installation of certain products is potentially disastrous. The biggest problems occur when materials designed for use with modern construction systems are used in old buildings; many of these act as a barrier to moisture and do not take account of the need for traditional structures to breathe.

The pressure to make thermal improvements is huge and the advice offered can be contradictory and confusing. For this reason, it is important to be well informed to recognise inappropriate products and unscrupulous salesmen. Understanding a little of the science will help you arrive at the right decision.

HOW OLD BUILDINGS LOSE HEAT

The external envelope of a building loses heat in two very different ways. Most noticeable is air leakage: gaps around windows and doors, cracks in walls, and junc-

Left: Gaps in and around doors and windows are a key area of heat loss.

Above: Thermal imaging is an ideal way of analysing areas of heat loss.

tions between different building elements allow warm air to escape and draughts (cold air) to penetrate. In addition, heat is lost through the building fabric itself, passing through walls, roofs, floors and even panes of glass due to thermal conductivity.

Air leakage and thermal conductivity must be analysed and addressed separately. Heat loss through draughts is much faster than heat loss via conductivity, therefore airtightness is more crucial than insulation. Insulation on its own will not necessarily provide airtightness.

Thermal conduction and resistivity

Heat passes through different building materials at different rates. Metal is a good thermal conductor, wood is not (so we use a wooden spoon rather than a metal spoon to stir the contents of a hot pan). Brick and stone fall somewhere in between and are moderately good thermal conductors. This means that the amount of heat lost through traditional walls depends on their thickness, density, moisture content and construction.

Thermal resistivity is the opposite of thermal conductivity and is sometimes used to illustrate the insulation value of a material. For example, insulating quilt has low thermal conductivity and high thermal resistivity. Generally, the thermal properties of a material are related to their density. Denser materials are able to conduct heat, whereas lightweight materials contain a high proportion of air and therefore resist the flow of heat.

Thermal bridging

When insulation is added to existing buildings, any weak points in the insulation layer will form concentrated areas of heat loss known as 'thermal bridges'. Where these occur, not only do they cause heat loss, but they also attract condensation. Whereas the uninsulated building spreads the condensation over large areas, in an insulated building any condensation will be focused at thermal bridges where the surface is relatively colder.

Examples of elements that provide thermal bridges include metal-framed windows, concrete floor slabs, steel lintels and metal fixings. For instance, screws penetrating insulated plasterboard will allow heat to bypass the insulation and act as a thermal bridge.

Air leakage

Sometimes referred to as 'air permeability', air leakage is the uncontrolled movement of air (draughts) through joints and gaps in a building's fabric and can be a significant source of heat loss.

When old houses are draughty this tends to be due to ill-fitting doors that may have sagged; doors with gaps beneath them because of uneven floors; windows so covered in thick layers of paint they no longer close properly and gaps opening up around infill panels in timber-frame structures. Some of these areas of air leakage may be easy to resolve through sensitive repair but the quest for airtightness often results in loss of historic features and inappropriate alterations.

Air leakage is driven by a pressure difference between the internal and external environments, either sucking in or pushing out air. The pressure difference is caused by three main factors:

> external wind around the building envelope, inducing positive and negative pressure
> heating, causing the warm air inside the building to rise
> mechanical ventilation, drawing air out of the building

Wherever air is lost from a building, or rises as a result of heating, it causes fresh air to be sucked in from outside in the form of draughts. The effect is most noticeable on cold windy days when the pressure differential between inside and outside is at its peak and the air being sucked in is much colder than the air that is lost. Extra energy is required to heat the fresh cold air, making a leaky house inefficient compared to a house that is airtight.

The terms air leakage and air permeability should not be confused with 'breathability' and 'vapour-permeability'. The latter terms are not air movement through a building's fabric, but the movement of water vapour; they are linked to the pore size and structure within the fabric itself. A building can be airtight and still be breathable.

Likewise, airtightness and insulation are two different things. A building may be airtight and have no gaps or cracks but, if the building envelope is poorly insulated, heat will be lost through the fabric due to conductivity. Equally, insulating a draughty building is going to produce limited results if measures are not first taken to reduce air leakage.

MEASURING HEAT LOSS

Heat loss due to conductivity, as well as key areas of air leakage, may be analysed using a thermal imaging camera. Air leakage is measured with an airtightness test. Importantly, both techniques are non-invasive to the building.

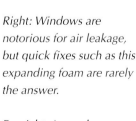

Above: Spreader plates in old walls act as thermal bridges. These can become problematic if walls are insulated.

Right: Windows are notorious for air leakage, but quick fixes such as this expanding foam are rarely the answer.

Far right: A membrane is taped at the edges and where ducting penetrates to maximise airtightness.

Above: A nineteenth-century brick cottage in Oxfordshire. The thermal image (right) reveals air leakage under the eaves and through the wall vents, and heat loss via the chimney stacks.

Thermal imaging

Infrared thermography or thermal imaging is used to detect the infrared radiation which is emitted by all objects: the warmer the object the more infrared radiation it emits. Thermal imaging cameras detect this radiation, and its varying levels are translated into a range of colours that correspond to the temperature of the objects being viewed. This means that heat loss, uninsulated areas and air leakage can be seen. Materials that have decayed, voids within the structure and moisture-saturated areas may also be detected.

Thermal imaging works best when a building is heated internally and the external temperature is cold, otherwise all surfaces may appear similar. Thermograms should be interpreted by experts and must generally be read in conjunction with visual surveys and other investigations of the structure. Without sufficient experience the images can be confusing. Contact your local authority or the SPAB for names of local thermal imaging firms.

This thermal image of a timber-framed house shows variations in heat loss across its facade. The white patches indicate areas of greatest heat loss, invariably through air leakage. Note the white spot under the gable verge, and draughts around the edges of windows. Red and then yellow are the next most thermally inefficient areas. Just above the front door, a red patch shows a radiator losing heat through the wall and the yellow patches to the roof indicate missing areas of insulation. The large inglenook chimney is losing considerable heat through its stack and the eaves are also poorly insulated. Thermal images of windows can be misleading, however, so interpretation requires care and experience.

Airtightness test

This is sometimes referred to as a 'blower door' test. The testing procedure involves sealing extractors, wall vents and chimneys, as well as trickle vents and flues. An external door is then opened and a temporary airtight screen with a fan is fitted into the frame. This is generally used to 'depressurise' or suck air out of the building, to create a pressure difference between the inside and outside of approximately 50 Pascals. The airflow through the fan and the pressure differences are then measured and the airtightness of the external envelope can be assessed. Alternatively, the building may be 'pressurised', depending on the circumstances. The test normally takes around an hour and during this time the house can be occupied as normal.

For new buildings, airtightness must meet the requirements of Building Regulations. For old buildings, the test provides a useful tool to analyse the level of draughts. Old buildings frequently perform better than expected, with air leakage problems often relating to alterations and extensions rather than the original fabric.

The assessment will give a measurement of air leakage but, even more usefully, while the fan is running, it is possible to pinpoint draughts that may not have been previously apparent. When the building is depressurised, it creates a lower internal pressure that sucks air in from outside through any gaps in the building fabric. If you run a damp finger or the back of your hand around junctions and penetrations, draughts can be detected. These points of air leakage should be marked and remedied in due course.

The level of airtightness is measured in $m^3/(h.m^2)$ at 50 Pa – in other words, the quantity of air (in m^3) which leaks out of the building per hour, divided by the total surface area of the building including party walls (in m^2) at 50 Pa of pressure difference. The lower the value achieved, the more airtight the dwelling.

Above and left: An airtightness test in progress.

Right: A smoke pencil, emitting non-toxic smoke, can also indicate air leakage while the fan is running.

MEASUREMENT TERMS EXPLAINED

A number of standard units of measurement for expressing insulation and heat loss properties are used:

k-values: 'k' is the coefficient of thermal conductivity. Every material has its own k-value and these can be used to compare the insulation properties of one product against another; the lower the value the better. For example, the k-value of sheep's wool insulation is typically 0.037, brick values range from around 0.6 to 1.3 depending on their type and density, while iron is 80. The lower figure for sheep's wool immediately shows that it is a much better insulator than brick; the high figure for iron indicates that it is a good thermal conductor, with virtually no insulation value. In the UK k-values are given in W/m.K (Watts per metre Kelvin).

U-values: Thermal transmissivity or U-values define the rate of heat transfer through a building component, for instance a wall, floor or roof. They are the standard way of expressing heat loss via thermal conductivity. For any given construction, the U-value is calculated using the k-value of each layer and its thickness. U-values are expressed in W/m²K (Watts per square metre Kelvin). The lower the U-value, the better the thermal efficiency of the building component. The higher the U-value, the more heat is lost and the less energy-efficient your home will be.

For example, the U-value of a traditional 9-inch (225mm) solid brick wall is around 2.7. This is calculated using a k-value of 0.6, divided by the wall thickness, 0.225m. Using the same k-value, a 13½-inch (338mm) solid brick wall has a U-value of 1.8 – the slightly thicker wall loses heat at a reduced rate. Whereas the U-value will vary according to the thickness of the wall, the k-value for a particular type of brick will remain constant.

To determine the U-value of a series of different layers, for instance in an insulated wall, the calculation becomes more complex, and the U-values of the individual layers cannot be simply added together.

Below: The k-value of brick is high compared to that of insulating materials such as cork. Confusingly, the R-value of brick is low, whereas that of cork is high.

Below: A timber-framed house with 4-inch (102mm) thick wattle and daub panels has a high U-value, with walls that are thermally inefficient. The thatched roof, with a low U-value, performs well.

Below: The cement render to the base of this wall has caused low-level internal damp. Here, it is removed and replaced with hydraulic lime.

R-values: The opposite, or reciprocal, of U-values, R-values express thermal resistivity for a material of a given thickness. Some product literature will give the R-value, rather than the U-value. In the case of insulating materials, a high R-value means a better insulator than a low R-value. Thermal resistance is measured in m^2K/W.

SAP and RdSAP: Standard Assessment Procedure (SAP) is the government's methodology for assessing and comparing the energy and environmental performance of new dwellings. Reduced Data SAP (RdSAP) was introduced in 2005 as a simpler, lower-cost method developed for existing dwellings. A wide range of detailed calculations and measurements are used to determine a final rating. SAP ratings are expressed on a scale of 1 to 100+. The higher the number, the better the rating; over 100 means the dwelling is a net producer of energy when considering heating/hot water and lighting. Most new homes achieve ratings of 80 or above.

MOISTURE AND MATERIALS

The science of why certain materials are breathable and others are not is complex. It is crucial to understand some of the basics before making decisions about how to repair and insulate an old building. The materials you choose will have a major impact on the way your house functions.

It has long been understood that damp problems are often exacerbated by attempts to keep moisture out through the inappropriate use of cement renders, plastic membranes and concrete floor slabs. In the quest for energy-efficiency, the addition of modern, impermeable insulation to the building envelope of old houses is likely to trap moisture and have the same disastrous consequences. This means it is essential to understand how traditional solid-walled buildings work, and to ensure that any intervention is compatible. The type of insulation used, coupled with the way it is fitted, is key to the health of both the building and its occupants.

BREATHABILITY

Breathability is a term that is widely used but rarely defined. In its strictest sense, breathability is the water vapour transmission rate, or the speed at which vapour passes through a particular material or construction. In a practical application, breathability is a combination of three important properties: vapour-permeability, hygroscopicity and capillarity.

Breathability has become a buzz word in the construction industry. In reality, many so-called breathable products have such little ability to diffuse water vapour that they remain entirely incompatible with traditional fabric.

Porosity and vapour-permeability

Porosity and vapour-permeability describe two very different properties of materials but are frequently confused. Porosity relates to the percentage of holes, or 'pores', within a material. vapour-permeability is the rate of passage of water vapour through a material, via the pores. Permeability is dependent on both the size of the pores and, crucially, whether they are linked or closed. A material can be highly porous, but completely impermeable – for instance, a sheet of closed-cell foam insulation. The closed pores will trap a great quantity of air, making them very good thermal insulators, but they will be a barrier to water vapour transmission.

Right, above: Breathing walls reach a natural moisture equilibrium but can be easily compromised through the use of inappropriate materials.

Right: Old bricks are highly porous and, because the pores are linked, vapour-permeable.

Vapour diffusion

The way water vapour travels through a vapour-permeable material is described as vapour diffusion. It is driven by the vapour pressure differential: the difference in vapour pressure between one side and the other. The internal environment of a house usually has a higher vapour pressure than the external, but this is not always the case: occasionally water vapour will travel from the outside inwards. Where a vapour barrier is present on the internal wall, it may trap moisture when this occurs.

Capillary action

Capillaries are interlinking pores in porous materials. When a porous brick is left in an inch of water it will quickly 'wick' or suck up the moisture: this is known as 'capillary action'. The amount of moisture it sucks up will be dependent on the capillarity of the brick: the pore size and the way the pores are connected. This is how rising damp occurs in walls with no physical damp-proof course when they are saturated at the base. A course of slate, a plastic membrane or an engineering brick provides a 'capillary break' to resist rising damp. The capillarity of the brick or stone with which your house was built is an important factor when detailing a wall insulation system.

Relative humidity and hygroscopicity

Relative humidity, or RH, is the amount of water vapour in the air relative to the maximum amount that can exist at that temperature. Air at a higher temperature can hold more water vapour, hence a warm room is less likely to be damp than a cold room. Not turning heating on to save money can be a false economy: the colder the internal temperature, the less able the air is to hold water vapour and RH will rise. Consequently soft furnishings will smell musty and go mouldy.

Retrospective damp-proof courses

Injected damp-proof courses are marketed as a way of retrospectively fitting a capillary break in the base of the wall by squeezing in silicone and expecting it to spread sideways to form an impermeable layer. In reality, it rarely works and is usually unnecessary, expensive and damaging. It is only guaranteed if combined with a hard cement tanking plaster on the inside face of the wall which traps moisture and masks the problem, leaving the wall damp and therefore thermally inefficient.

Low-level dampness in solid-walled, breathing structures can usually be resolved by dealing with the cause of damp, allowing the wall to dry out and then repairing with permeable lime-based mortars and plasters.

Below: This retrospective damp-proof course has been injected into the bricks, but will almost certainly have no effect.

Above: Test the capillarity of a material by placing it in water to see how much is wicked up.

Left: Condensation is particularly noticeable on windows in bedrooms and bathrooms where the relative humidity is high.

Right: Clay plasters and breathable paints play a useful role in hygroscopic buffering.

Ventilation generally reduces RH by swapping internal damp-laden air for fresh air from outside. This assumes, however, that the external RH is lower than the internal RH – and that is not always the case on a damp, humid day. In this instance, a powerful extractor fan will do more good than opening a window. Ideally, RH should be between 40 and 60 per cent for good internal air quality. Once RH is above 73 per cent, mould and dust mites will thrive and pose a serious threat to human health (➡ Wellbeing, page 32).

Hygroscopicity refers to the ability of a material to absorb and release water vapour. A hygroscopic material will readily absorb excess vapour as the relative humidity in the room increases, and will release it as the RH falls.

Hygroscopic buffering

Activities such as showering and drying clothes all increase the relative humidity within a house. In a draughty building, this will be naturally reduced due to ventilation but, as we make buildings more airtight, the hygroscopic abilities of the materials we use become more important. Many natural insulation products and clay plasters in particular are able to absorb and store excess water vapour, reducing the RH when it is high and bringing it back down to safe limits. This stabilising effect is referred to as hygroscopic buffering, and will reduce condensation and mould growth.

CONDENSATION AND DEWPOINT

Condensation occurs when water vapour in the air makes contact with a cold surface and condenses, returning to a liquid. The temperature at which it condenses is called the dewpoint. This is often noticeable on cold external walls, uninsulated ceilings and poorly ventilated corners of rooms behind cupboards where air circulation is minimal. Condensation also forms on areas where thermal bridging is present. The higher the relative humidity, the more moisture is present in the air and the more likely condensation is to occur.

Condensation can lead to the formation of mould growth on surfaces. *Aspergillus niger* is particularly common and is readily identified by a patch of small black spots. This mould prefers pure condensed water, hence it is a good indicator of condensation rather than any other form of damp. Rising and penetrating damp usually carry salts from either the building fabric or the ground so therefore do not usually provide appropriate conditions for this type of mould.

Right: Unventilated cupboards on external walls are particularly prone to condensation and mould.

Interstitial condensation

Water is the biggest enemy of old buildings and keeping the rain out has long been a preoccupation. But water in the form of vapour, passing from the internal environment and condensing within the wall, remains invisible and is therefore regularly overlooked.

During the colder months, there is a big temperature difference between the internal and external wall surface. Somewhere in between, within the body of the wall itself, the temperature is at dewpoint – and when vapour hits dewpoint it will condense. This is known as interstitial condensation.

Analysis

The risk of interstitial condensation has traditionally been calculated using Glaser diagrams. These were developed in the 1950s to analyse the experimental techniques of lightweight construction that were appearing at the time. Glaser diagrams are relatively easy to use: they have two inputs, the thermal conductivity of each material and its vapour-permeability. They assume that the wall is always kept dry and protected from rain. This is not always the case with old buildings, as breathing walls allow moisture, both as vapour and as liquid (i.e. rain) to move through the structure, and so moisture levels are constantly changing due to changing use patterns and weather. The Glaser diagram is not able to consider all the complex factors involved in a breathing wall (and indeed in any wall), such as the capillary and hygroscopic qualities of materials, driving rain and solar drying.

A far more accurate risk analysis can be carried out by using a dynamic 'hygrothermal simulation' that takes into account all the qualities of building fabric and the conditions to which they are subjected. Such simulations should conform to EN 15026, for example WUFI (Wärme und Feuchte instationär) or Delphin software. These models consider a whole range of factors in a dynamic state and produce far more accurate modelling, albeit that many of the material data for traditional buildings are still not properly known and the performance of traditional buildings is difficult to model accurately because of the complexity of the fabric.

Many manufacturers and specifiers continue to use the over-simplistic Glaser analysis. This can lead to misleading results and potentially inappropriate choices, particularly for older buildings.

MEMBRANES AND BARRIERS

There is much confusion over the different membranes available and where they should be used.

Non-woven geotextile membrane: a strong, bonded fibre sheet that allows liquid and vapour to pass easily through while blocking larger particles. It is commonly used under paths and patios to deter weeds, or for drainage purposes to prevent soakaways and French drains from silting up.

Timber decay

Old buildings invariably contain embedded timbers such as joist ends, bonding timbers and lintels. Provided these remain relatively dry, and the moisture content low, few problems are likely to occur. For a safe working figure, a moisture content of around 12 per cent is often quoted. Where timber becomes damp due to building defects, driving rain or interstitial condensation, its moisture content will rise and it becomes vulnerable to dry rot and beetle infestation.

For many years there has been a common misconception that chemicals can eradicate timber decay and beetle infestation. Yet practical experience and scientific study have indicated that the best way to overcome such outbreaks is simply to dry out the timber and reduce the moisture content to within safe limits. Despite overwhelming evidence to support this advice, a chemical timber treatment industry has grown up offering questionable 'solutions' and guarantees, often insisted upon by mortgage providers.

Chemicals are rarely necessary or effective against timber decay. Furthermore, blanket spraying without good justification is contrary to regulations on the Control of Substances Hazardous to Health. In fact, spiders are the best natural predator of beetles – yet they are killed by chemicals. If necessary, while timber is drying out, a localised treatment with borax may help control outbreaks of beetles; this is a naturally occurring mineral with preservative and insect-repellent properties.

Left: Embedded joist ends are vulnerable to decay if walls are damp. Here, chemical treatment is being applied but this cannot reach the end grain of the joist where moisture absorption is at its greatest.

Breathable membrane: also known as a vapour-permeable membrane, this is a finely perforated sheeting material that allows water vapour to pass through, but does not allow the passage of water droplets.

These are generally installed on the cold side of insulation, where some level of waterproofing is required, but where the easy passage of water vapour is important to prevent the build-up of moisture in the wall as in interstitial condensation. Typically, they are employed under roof tiles or behind external cladding. There is some concern that the pores of such membranes become blocked over time and vapour-permeability is reduced.

Vapour control layer (VCL): where insulation is added internally, a VCL or vapour check is used on the warm side of the insulation. This prevents the majority of the water vapour passing through the insulation and condensing within the thickness of the building envelope as interstitial condensation.

Vapour barrier: where a construction system relies on no water vapour passing through, a vapour barrier is used. This has a high vapour resistance but it is dangerous to rely completely on this. In practice, such membranes can rarely achieve 100 per cent vapour tightness due to imperfect workmanship and punctures from services.

Damp-proof membrane (DPM): usually a strong, impermeable plastic membrane laid under concrete floors to resist rising damp.

VENTILATION

While airtightness is critical to make a building thermally efficient, ventilation remains equally important to control relative humidity levels. Approximately 0.4 to 0.5 air changes per hour (ac/h) are recommended in modern homes. This equates to 40 per cent of the total volume of air within the building being replaced every hour. In a solid-walled traditional building, up to 0.8 ac/h may be needed due to the extra moisture present within the building structure. If a building is damp, ventilation should be increased even further to keep RH levels down.

Ideally, ventilation should be controlled rather than being allowed to occur randomly due to air leakage and draughts. Control might be by simply opening a window for ten minutes, or through mechanical means.

THERMAL INSULATION

Adding thermal insulation to roofs, floors and walls will, in theory, reduce heat loss via conductivity and make your home more thermally efficient. But choosing materials carefully and maintaining high standards of workmanship are crucial to success. Insulation on its own does not necessarily provide airtightness; it may need to be combined with other products to provide a total solution.

Choosing materials

Often a varied palette of insulation materials must be employed in a single building to achieve the highest thermal standards and the most appropriate solutions across all areas. Some materials are thin and highly insulating so are ideal where space is limited; others are cheaper but a greater thickness is required to achieve the equivalent performance. This can be readily assessed by comparing the k-value of each.

Think carefully before insulating older buildings because of the risk of damp and decay. Breathable insulation materials ensure that moisture does not become trapped while hygroscopic materials act as moisture buffers by absorbing and releasing water vapour.

Left: Natural insulation materials come in various forms.

Below: One of the considerations with insulation materials is ease of cutting and fitting.

Insulation comes in quilts (rolls), batts (slabs), boards or as loose fill. Spray foams are also available. Quilt rolls provide long lengths. Batts are made up of shorter, firmer, more manageable lengths. Boards are ideal where a rigid material is required. Loose-fill or blown insulation is usually pumped in by professional installers and, by its nature, fills every nook and cranny, even around pipework and wiring, although it can settle over time. In addition, a number of composite products are available in which insulation is combined with other materials such as plasterboard. Pipework is generally lagged with slit or semi-slit insulation tubes.

When buying insulation materials check how they should be cut. Generally, with roll, batt and quilt materials, it is better to measure them for size and then cut them with a saw or a knife than to tear them apart, but bear in mind that blades tend to be quickly blunted.

Left: Areas where insulation has been poorly installed become apparent in snow.

Material choice

When selecting insulation material there are a number of key points to consider depending on your priorities and the situation in which it is to be used:

> Does it need to be breathable?
> Will it provide the thermal performance required?
> Is there sufficient space for it to be installed?
> How practical and easy is it to use?
> Can it be cut and fixed appropriately?
> Is the cost affordable and justified?
> Are you keen to use natural products?
> Is the material recyclable at the end of its life?
> What is its embodied energy and carbon?
> Is acoustic insulation required?

Below: There are a wide variety of materials available, so take advice and choose the one best suited to your home.

Above: Spray foams may seem like a good solution, but are often a false economy in the longer term.

Right: Care needs to be taken when fixing insulation materials since metal fixings such as screws and nails that penetrate insulation materials may cause a thermal bridge. Where necessary, use specially designed thermally broken fixings that are intended to protect against this problem.

Quick fixes

Spray foams applied directly to walls, roofs and floors to provide thermal insulation and airtightness, and to consolidate unsound surfaces, pose potential risks when used in old buildings. Although some manufacturers claim that these products are formulated to reduce the risk of condensation and mould, the danger of moisture being trapped is very real. This is particularly concerning where timber is present as decay is likely to result.

In the event of failure spray foams are not easily removed, so problems will be difficult to rectify without damage to the fabric of the building. This also means that the salvage of building materials, such as roofing slates and tiles, for reuse will be difficult in the future.

Among other products being sold as quick and easy insulation solutions are flexible thermal linings. These are typically around 10mm thick and are pasted to the wall in a similar way to wallpaper. As with foam, they are not recommended for use on old walls that need to breathe.

Health and safety

When using insulation materials, always follow manufacturer's instructions as some can cause severe irritation to the skin, eyes and respiratory tract. Depending on the product, face masks, gloves and protective clothing may be necessary. Natural materials are generally less problematic.

When working in loft spaces use kneeling boards to bridge joists and be aware of the potentially fragile nature of old ceilings. Always try to avoid burying cables under insulation materials as there is a danger that they may overheat and pose a fire risk.

Buying insulation checklist

Before buying an insulation system, do your research. Speak to the manufacturer's technical adviser, or ask a potential supplier the following questions:

> Do they have experience in advising on breathable structures?
> Are they able to carry out a condensation risk analysis?
> Is the condensation risk analysis based on Glaser or a hygrothermal simulation such as WUFI? Avoid any analysis based on Glaser, as it is unlikely to provide accurate modelling of an old building.
> Are they able to supply a detailed written specification?
> Can the system offer a guarantee against interstitial condensation?
> Is it tried and tested in this particular application?
> If it is advertised as a breathable product, what does this mean – has it been quantified?

Right: Homebuilding exhibitions are a good place to find out more about products.

Insulation materials

GENERIC PRODUCT	Blown	Boards/batts	Rolls	Pour	Thermal performance	Embodied energy	Cost range	mm thickness required to achieve U-value of 0.25 Wm²K	Flat roof over joists	Flat roof between joists	Pitched roof over rafters	Pitched roof between rafters	Ceiling level	Cavity wall (full fill)	Cavity wall (partial fill)	Exterior wall	Within structural frame	Suspended timber floors	Solid concrete floor
Natural products																			
cellulose	●		●		▨	■	▨	150		●		●	●					●	●
cork (expanded)		●			▨	■	▨	160	●	●	●	●			1	●		●	●
cotton			●		▨	▨	▨	160		●		●	●					●	●
flax			●		▨	▨	▨	170		●		●	●					●	●
hemp			●		▨	▨	▨	175		●		●	●					●	●
monolithic lime/hemp mix[2]				●	■	▨[3]	■	260									●	●	
reed board		●			▨	▨	▨	220					●					●	
sheep's wool		●			▨	▨	▨	150		●		●	●					●	●
wood fibreboard[4]		●			▨	▨	▨	150	●	●	●	●	●				●	●	●
Mineral products																			
aerogel		●			■	■	■	55						●		●	●	●	
calcium silicate board		●			▨	▨	■	n/a									●		
cellular glass		●			▨	▨	▨	160	●		●			●	●	●			●
glass fibre	●	●			▨	▨	▨	150		●		●	●	●	●	●	●		
lightweight expanded clay				●	■	▨		350											●
stone mineral wool	●	●			▨	▨	▨	150		●		●	●	●	●	●	●	●	
vermiculite				●	■	■	▨	250		●			●					●	
Petrochemical																			
expanded polystyrene		●			▨	■	▨	125	●	●	●	●		●	●	●	●	●	●
extruded polystyrene		●			▨	■	▨	110	●	●	●	●		●	●	●	●	●	●
phenolic foam boards		●			■	■	▨	80			●	●			●		●	●	●
polyurethane		●			▨	■	▨	80	●	●	●	●			●		●	●	●
recycled plastic fibre wool			●		▨	▨	▨	175			●	●					●	●	
Composites																			
multifoils[5]		●			■	■	▨	n/a	●	●	●	●	●						
vacuum insulated panels		●			■	▨	■	25		●		●	●				●	●	●	●

Key		Thermal performance (k-value, W/mK)	Embodied energy (MJ/kg)
■ ▨ ▨ ▨ ■		■ > 0.45	> 50
Worst ➡ Best		▨ 0.36–0.44	30–49
		▨ 0.3–0.35	20–29
		▨ 0.26–0.29	10–19
		■ < 0.25	< 9

The chart compares the main types of insulation products available, showing the form they take and common uses as well as a guide to their relative thermal performance, embodied energy and cost.

Values indicated are averages across generic product types and are not manufacturer-specific figures. Actual performance may vary depending on individual manufacturer's products.

The method of assessing embodied energy is based on energy consumed in joules per kilogram of material and relates to end use within the UK.

There are alternative methods of assessing embodied energy, such as kilograms of carbon emitted per cubic metre of material, which can better reflect the fact that some materials with high embodied energy are very light and occupy a small amount of space. The method adopted here was chosen on the basis that there is a greater quantity of data available to allow a broader comparison of materials.

Notes
1. Not used in UK but known in Europe.
2. Monolithic lime/hemp mix cannot be directly compared with other insulation materials as it is a quasi-construction material rather than purely an insulant. The thermal value quoted is after 12 months' drying time at a density of 275 kg/m³. The embodied energy performance is better under other forms of carbon assessment.
3. Performs better under other forms of carbon assessment.
4. Depending on density.
5. Requires supplementary insulation.

Chart prepared by Conker Conservation Ltd

NATURAL INSULATION MATERIALS

Made from renewable or recyclable materials, natural insulation products usually allow the building's fabric to breathe and have excellent hygroscopic properties which assist in buffering changes in relative humidity. They are generally biodegradable or recyclable at the end of their life and safe to install with minimal protective clothing.

Cellulose: produced from recycled newspaper and other wastepaper; formaldehyde-, VOC- and CFC-free; sequesters CO_2; offers low air permeability.

Cork (expanded): harvested every 7–11 years from cork oak; dimensionally stable; can be plastered directly for external wall insulation.

Cotton: made from scrap/recycled material; good moisture-control properties.

Flax: produced from fibres of the linseed plant; sequesters CO_2; has good moisture-control properties.

Hemp: during growing little or no pesticides are needed, the soil is replenished with nutrients and nitrogen, and erosion of the topsoil is controlled; sequesters CO_2; offers good moisture-control properties.

Monolithic lime/hemp mix: composite material made from hemp shiv and lime-based binder; takes 12 months to reach optimum thermal performance due to drying time; sequesters CO_2; creates a very stable internal thermal and hygroscopic environment.

Reed board or mat: made from reeds held together using stainless or galvanized wire; breathable; especially useful for insulating timber-frame buildings.

Sheep's wool: hygroscopic/moisture buffering so will absorb water while remaining an efficient insulant; can help maintain the temperature above dewpoint; absorbs formaldehyde, detoxifying air.

Wood fibreboard: made from waste forest products and recycled timber with natural wood resins to bond particles together; breathable, vapour-permeable and hygroscopic; is sometimes impregnated or coated with paraffin wax, latex or bitumen to enhance moisture-resistance and durability.

Right: Natural insulation materials have many advantages over synthetic products.

MINERAL INSULATION MATERIALS

Although based on naturally occurring materials, extraction and production processes can be damaging to the environment. Some products offer breathability; not all are biodegradable or recyclable.

With certain materials, such as glass fibre quilts, problems occur when they become wet, as they slump and the air pockets fill with water, negating their insulation properties.

Aerogel: made by extracting water from silica gel and replacing it with CO_2; composed of 90 per cent air; slim profile makes it ideal for use where space is at a premium.

Calcium silicate board: manufactured by combining sand and lime in an autoclave under heat and steam pressure; microporous material; high capillary action ensures humidity regulation.

Cellular glass: contains up to 60 per cent recycled glass; dimensionally stable; high compressive strength.

Glass fibre: made from glass, a product of silica; can contain 30–60 per cent recycled content; compression occurs over time and reduces performance.

Lightweight expanded clay aggregate: granular and with a high natural content; available with silicon coating to make it waterproof.

Stone mineral wool: the majority of products use approximately 97 per cent virgin rock material with the remaining 3 per cent resin. Some use up to 75 per cent recycled mineral (slag) wool.

Vermiculite: naturally occurring mineral expanded at high temperatures to produce particles; pre-1990 vermiculite mined in Canada was found to be contaminated with asbestos.

Above: Builders often fail to wear protective clothing when using mineral insulation products, putting themselves at risk.

PETROCHEMICAL INSULATION MATERIALS

Petrochemical-derived materials embody both resource depletion and pollution risks from oil and plastics production. Products are non-biodegradable and may create toxic fumes when burnt.

Expanded polystyrene (EPS): sometimes contains graphite to reflect heat radiation, so is silver-grey in appearance, with an improved k-value; direct contact with PVC cables should be avoided as plasticizers in PVC may migrate into EPS causing it to shrink and the cables to become brittle.

Extruded polystyrene (XPS): denser and stronger than EPS; highly resistant to water absorption; as with EPS, direct contact with PVC cables should be avoided.

Phenolic foam boards: very low conductivity; often faced with foil which may block wi-fi or other transmitted signals.

Polyurethane (PUR), polyisocyanurate (PIR) board and spray foam: very low conductivity; board products often faced with foil which may block wi-fi or other transmitted signals.

Recycled plastic bottle fibre wool: manufactured from 85 per cent recycled plastic bottles, 15 per cent polyester.

COMPOSITE INSULATION MATERIALS

These are made up of various elements to provide specialised solutions where the use of other products may not be possible.

Multi-foils: multi-layer insulation with aluminium bonded to both surfaces; lightweight, flexible and thin; may block wi-fi or other transmitted signals.

Vacuum insulated panels (VIPs): open porous core material with a gas-tight envelope to maintain quality of the vacuum; highly sensitive to mechanical impact – if vacuum seal is broken, panel performance is reduced.

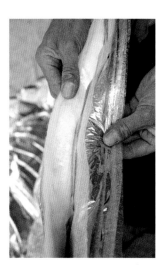

Left: Foil-faced foam boards offer excellent k-values but are generally not breathable.

Above: Ever more complex insulation materials such as multi-foils are becoming available. These may have applications in specific instances, but tend to overcomplicate traditional construction.

Roofs and ceilings

Since hot air rises, it makes sense that roofs should be a high priority when improving a building's thermal efficiency. Adding loft insulation is a relatively easy and cost-effective task; insulating attic rooms and sloping ceilings tends to be more complex.

Traditionally the main purpose of a roof has been to keep the elements out; keeping heat in has tended to be a secondary consideration. Today a roof has to perform in all respects: it must resist wind and rain and it should incorporate a high level of thermal insulation and airtightness. It might even be green in every sense of the word and a place where plants are grown to encourage biodiversity.

Energy-efficiency campaigns have frequently focused on persuading homeowners to upgrade their loft insulation. Often this work is inexpensive and straightforward and has a relatively quick payback period because of the reduction to energy bills that it achieves. Despite this, many homes still have surprisingly poorly insulated roof spaces. Others have seen ill-conceived insulation strategies that are at best inefficient and, at worst, hugely damaging to the building's fabric.

Incorporating insulation into an old roof and reducing air leakage from the rooms below rely on using appropriate methods and materials. An empty loft space must be treated in a very different way to an attic containing living accommodation, while an ancient timber-framed roof may need a solution totally at odds with a loft conversion in a Victorian terrace. Any solution needs to take account of condensation resulting from water vapour as this can cause major problems if left to chance.

Opposite: Where roofs fail, the whole building is at risk.

Left: Roofs can become energy generators, but sometimes at the expense of aesthetics.

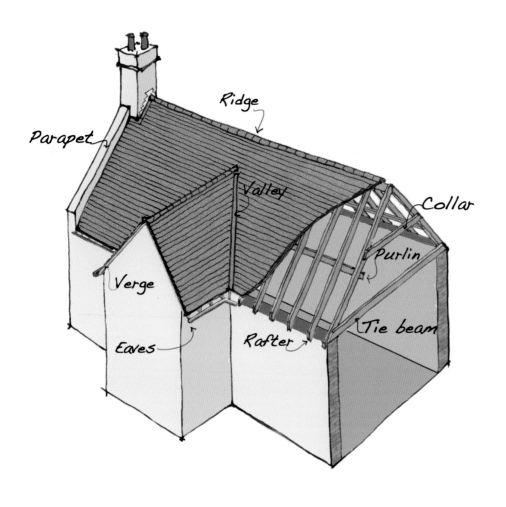

Above: The principal elements of a roof.

Right: Re-tiling will generally require Building Regulations approval.

BUILDING REGULATIONS

Under the Building Regulations, roofs to existing buildings must be upgraded to comply with current U-values under the circumstances listed on page 29, and, more specifically:

> when the roof space is being converted to a habitable room (but not if the habitable room already exists)

> when more than 50 per cent of the roof is to be re-roofed

Even if the circumstances above apply, a thermal upgrade is only required if the existing U-value is greater than the 'threshold U-value'.

WHAT TO CONSIDER

Always establish the best way to insulate your particular roof from the outset and discuss technical solutions with manufacturers and suppliers, but beware of advice that is not impartial. If necessary, appoint an architect or surveyor with an understanding of traditional, breathable structures to inspect the roof fully. Where there is any doubt, it may be better to leave the roof without insulation. Numerous factors should be considered before insulating roof spaces, including:

> Are you planning to leave the roof space 'cold'? Insulation at ceiling level is by far the easiest and cheapest option.

> How is the roof ventilated and is there a condensation problem?

> Is the roof space occupied or are you planning a loft conversion in the future? Plan ahead and think carefully how to best insulate the roof.

> Is the roof in poor condition? If so, it may be more economical to re-roof and insulate at the same time.

> Will insulation raise the line of the roof? Carefully consider the implications.

> Is there a danger of thermal bridging due to dormers, parapets or valley gutters? Never leave your roofer to find a solution to these details.

> Is the roof an historic structure and does it contain torching (plastering to the underside of the tiles or slates)? If so, more sensitive solutions will be required.

> Will the work be above fragile historic ceilings? Screws rather than nails will minimise vibration.

Above left: Are solar panels to be added? Check the suitability of the structure in advance (➠ Roof-mounted panels, page 160).

Above: Dormers are problematic when rafter-level insulation is undertaken.

The three principal types of roof space

Cold roof

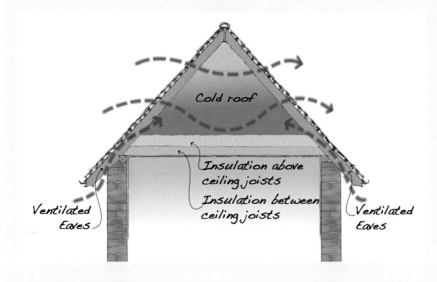

A clear ventilated roof space which remains uninhabited and where the rafters are exposed on the underside. In such cases, loft insulation is a simple matter of choosing a suitable material to lay above the ceiling of the habitable rooms below (➡ Horizontal ceiling insulation, page 62).

The photograph shows a typical Scottish cold roof space with sarking boards over the rafters.

Semi-occupied roof

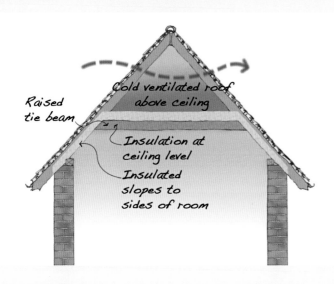

A combination of a warm roof and a cold roof, typical in cottages. The tie beams are raised to give the habitable room below more headroom, resulting in areas of sloping or 'coombed' ceiling, while the loft space above remains cold. The insulation strategy should consider the height of the walls in relation to the area of sloping ceiling.

The photograph shows a cottage bedroom with a coombed or sloping section of ceiling which, unless the roof is thatched, is notoriously difficult to insulate.

Warm roof

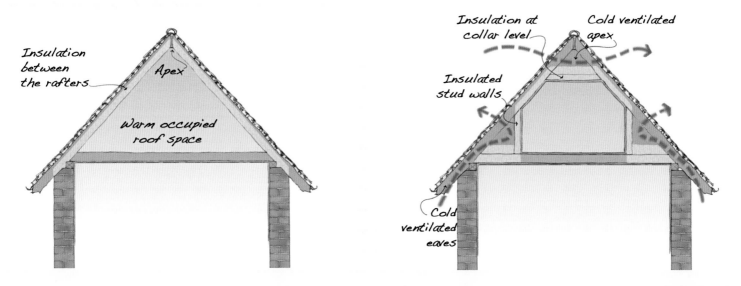

An insulated roof space that contains an attic room or loft conversion. The insulation is along the rafter line and the habitable space is sometimes clear to the apex and the eaves at the sides (above far left). More commonly (above) stud walls have been constructed to create a vertical wall, with an eaves void behind, and the collars have been plastered forming a small area of flat ceiling. If the house was originally designed this way, the plasterwork may be historic lath and plaster. Alternatively, the loft space may have been converted into a habitable room in recent years (➠ Rafter-level insulation, page 65).

The photograph is of an original attic room in a nineteenth-century house. The low vertical wall to the left is a stud partition with lath and plaster finish, containing an eaves void behind.

Safety first

When working in roof spaces always think about safety:

> Dress in appropriate clothing and footwear and consider wearing kneeling pads.
> Although not necessarily required with natural insulation materials, it is always sensible to wear a good-quality face mask and gloves. Loft spaces are frequently dusty and may contain old insulation materials, asbestos, as well as the remains of wildlife and bird, bat and rodent droppings.
> Ensure there is sufficient light to work and carry a torch.
> Check you have safe access and that ladders are properly secured.
> Before stepping into the space, ensure it is safe to do so and that the joists are sound and are able to carry your weight. Never walk between the joists.
> Carry a mobile phone and let someone know that you are up there.

HORIZONTAL CEILING INSULATION

For cold roofs where roof spaces are unoccupied, insulation is generally laid above the ceiling. This is usually a simple operation, provided the ceiling and ceiling structure is sound.

Before you start

> Use a large board to spread your weight over several joists, taking care not to let it tip up on unsupported edges.
> Check the space for bats and nesting birds. Where they are present, you may have to modify how or when you carry out the work as they are protected by law (➡ Wildlife and buildings, page 179).
> It is often worth creating permanent access down the centre of the roof space by fitting 'crawl boards'. These should be raised to allow adequate insulation to be laid beneath, plus 50mm of ventilation to the underside of the board.
> Before laying any insulation, clean the space, removing any items or debris.

Top: An abandoned bird's nest is cleared from an old roof space before insulating.

Centre: Take care not to damage ceiling plaster 'nibs' when working from above.

Above: Insulating material must not be squashed to fit the space, as this will seriously compromise its effectiveness.

> It is usually best to remove and discard old insulation and start again, but find out first what it is – certain materials such as asbestos, fibreglass and fibrous vermiculite are hazardous and should not be handled unless precautions are taken to avoid breathing in the dust. If in doubt, call in a specialist to make tests and deal with removal.
> Take care not to damage the upper surface of your plaster ceiling when cleaning or working above. If you have a lath and plaster ceiling, the 'nibs' of the plaster should be visible protruding through the gaps and gripping the laths. These are important as they support the ceiling, so care should be taken not to break them off.
> Where older electrical installations are present, take the opportunity to get the system checked while the roof space is clear.
> Try to ensure all first-fix electrical work has been completed and, where possible, position any electrical junction boxes where they can be accessed without disturbing the insulation once it has been laid. Any future disturbance of the insulation will almost certainly reduce its effectiveness. Electricians are renowned for lifting quilts and only partially putting them back, leaving gaps and voids beneath.
> Where possible, cables should not run under insulation because of the fire risk from overheating.

Above: Laying sheep's wool in a roof space.

> If mechanical ventilation with heat recovery (MVHR) is being installed, this should be done before insulation is added, especially if the unit is in the roof space. Gaps around ductwork will need to be sealed appropriately to achieve airtightness where they pass through ceilings.

> Recessed light fittings should be carefully detailed (➡ Recessed light fittings, page 163).

> Seal the gaps around any pipes, cables and fittings that penetrate the ceiling structure, especially over kitchens and bathrooms. This will minimise air leakage and water vapour leading to condensation.

There are two main forms of material used to insulate above a flat, horizontal ceiling. The first comes as a quilt or a batt, either a manufactured product such as mineral wool, or a natural product such as sheep's wool or hemp. The second commonly used form comes as a loose fill. A rigid board is not recommended as it is difficult to cut exactly to size between joists, particularly irregular ones, leaving gaps around the edges (➡ Choosing materials, page 49).

Laying insulation quilt

> Choose a good-quality product, ideally one that is hygroscopic and able to absorb moisture vapour without slumping. Natural quilts are generally superior to man-made materials.

> The quilt thickness should achieve a minimum U-value of 0.16 and will vary according to the product used. Ask your supplier what thickness is required for that particular product.

> When fitting the quilt between joists, buy a product that comes in the correct width where possible to save cutting.

> If the joists are random widths apart, as is common in old buildings, it is important to cut, rather than rip, the quilt carefully, slightly wider than the space, to ensure there are no gaps around the edges. Ask your supplier to suggest a method of cutting the quilt and ensure you have the correct tools.

> The quilt should lie flat on the top of the ceiling, minimising air voids.

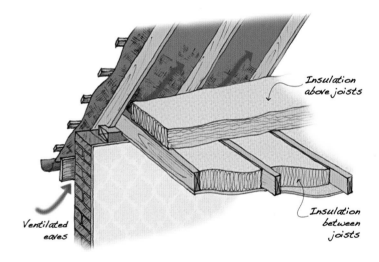

Above right: Quilts or batts are laid between joists, minimising any air gaps. Make up the necessary thickness with a second layer, laid at 90 degrees to the first. Continue the quilt right to the edge to minimise thermal bridging, but maintain an air gap at the eaves for ventilation.

Right: Tanks in roofs should be carefully sealed and insulated.

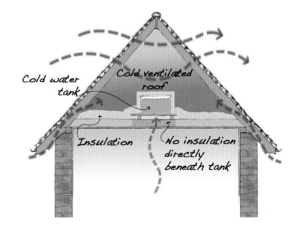

> The roof eaves are often poorly detailed but this is an important area to get right, otherwise thermal bridging and mould growth is likely to occur. Insulation should be continued to the eaves and, if possible, run over the wallplate and down the rafters, but this should not block eaves ventilation.

> Separate the insulation from any damp masonry or chimney stacks using a vapour-permeable membrane.

> Once laid, cover the insulation with a breathable membrane or building paper, taping any overlaps, to keep it clean from debris and dust. This will also assist with airtightness.

Laying loose-fill insulation above a ceiling

Various loose-fill insulation products are available. Perlite and vermiculite granules were commonly used in the 1970s, and are often found in old attic spaces, but have largely been replaced by cheaper alternatives. Cellulose fibre insulation produced from recycled newspaper has particularly good eco credentials. It does not have such a long lifespan as most insulation quilts but is more economical and often used in large loft spaces. The insulation is pumped in via a long hose to fill the space between and over joists up to the required thickness. Generally a settled thickness of 217mm will achieve a U-value of 0.16.

Loose-fill insulation is not recommended where the roof void is very draughty, as there is a high chance that the fill will be blown around, leading to varying thicknesses of insulation. Cellulose fibre insulation (recycled newspaper) is not suitable for roof spaces where it is likely to get damp.

Right: Where non-breathable felts are being retained, use small lengths of wood, typically 150mm long, with a screw sticking out, and push down between the lapped edges of the felt. This will create a series of gaps to assist with ventilation and minimise condensation.

Top: Proprietary roof venting system.

Above: New tiles being laid over breathable roofing felt.

Roof ventilation

Ventilation is crucial in roof spaces, otherwise condensation may form which can lead to decay of timber roof structures if left unchecked.

By the mid-twentieth century, non-breathable bituminous felts were being incorporated under slates and tiles. This system relied on a ventilated roof space beneath, otherwise they were vulnerable to condensation forming on the underside due to warm moist air rising and hitting the felt's cold surface. In recent years, breathable roofing felts have become the norm. These block liquid water from above but allow water vapour to pass through them from below, provided they are fitted correctly. In reality, they are often poorly installed, resulting in condensation, so always check the manufacturer's instructions and do not rely on your roofer to do so. Depending on the roof covering, breathable felts may not require eaves or ridge ventilation, although this may be a risky strategy where there are high levels of moisture vapour.

Regardless of the felt used, the first step is to avoid condensation problems by minimising the moisture vapour reaching the roof – for example, by installing seals around loft hatches. It may also be necessary to fix vents through the tiles or slates, particularly if they are profiled, machine-made or fit very closely with minimal gaps.

There are a variety of under-tile venting systems which can be slipped into position without stripping the roof, or incorporated during re-roofing. Some systems are more visually intrusive than others, so shop around to find the most inconspicuous product when viewing the roof from the ground. Eaves and ridge ventilators may also be necessary to encourage maximum cross-ventilation.

If you are stripping the roof and recovering or creating a room in the roof you may be required to fit roof ventilation under the Building Regulations. Ask your building control officer for advice.

Creating storage areas in loft spaces

Take care not to overload your joist structure with heavy storage boxes as this can cause deflection to roof timbers, cracking to the ceilings below and even collapse. If using your loft space for storage:

> Where possible, design a storage platform that is independent of the joists below and instead bears on load-bearing walls or beams. Leave a gap between the top of the ceiling and the underside of the storage deck – this will allow a good thickness of insulation to be added.
> Leave a 50mm gap between the underside of the deck and the top of the insulation.
> Avoid storage of flammable materials and always fit a hard-wired smoke alarm.
> Try to limit the weight of the items stored.

Below: Unoccupied roof spaces are frequently used for storage, but the weight of items should be limited. Access for maintenance and regular inspection is crucial.

RAFTER-LEVEL INSULATION

For warm roofs, where roof spaces have been converted to habitable rooms, the insulation is fitted to the sloping pitch along the line of the rafters. There are various ways of installing insulation, either above the rafters, below the rafters, in between the rafters or a combination of these. The best position technically, but not necessarily aesthetically, is above the rafters but this can only be done by carefully stripping the tiles or slates, usually as part of a re-roofing project. If you are not re-roofing your building, insulation to the slopes can only be fitted from inside the loft space.

Before embarking on any roof insulation, ask yourself, 'How long before this roof needs stripping and re-tiling?' If the roof's future life is relatively short, it may be better to opt for the long-term solution: strip the roof, insulate above the rafters and re-tile the entire area.

Rafter-level insulation from above

Insulation above the rafters is commonly referred to as 'sarking' insulation and is technically the best solution as it minimises the risk of condensation. It also minimises any disturbance to the attic space, as all the work can be carried out from above. This is an important consideration if the roof space is already plastered on the underside, either with modern or historic plaster. Importantly, it also allows for a continuous unbroken layer of insulation to be fitted that will be largely free from thermal bridging.

Above: An attic bedroom with rafter-level insulation.

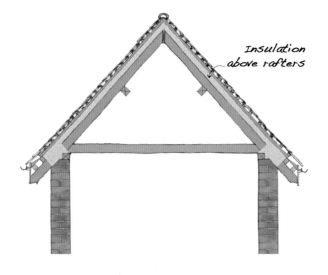

Insulation above rafters

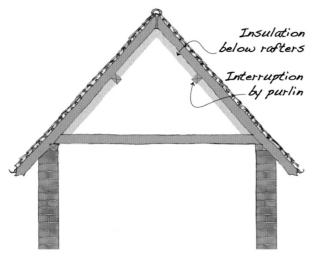

Insulation below rafters

Interruption by purlin

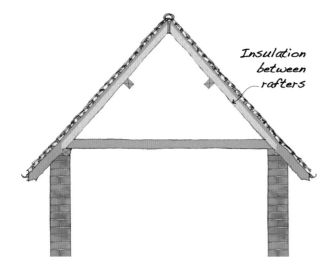

Insulation between rafters

Left: When roofs are insulated along the line of the rafters, careful consideration should be given to the position and type of insulation used.

Above: Insulation above the rafters takes time, and leaves the roof vulnerable while the covering is off. A temporary roof is often recommended to safeguard the rooms below.

This method of insulation does come with visual consequences. The thickness of the insulation will raise the level of the roof covering, changing the detail at the eaves and the verge typically by 100mm. It will also raise the height of the ridge and therefore potentially pose problems, including the need for party wall agreements on semi-detached and terraced houses, unless the adjoining roofs are similarly treated. Multi-foil systems (see below) may overcome some of these problems but are not suitable for every application. Non-combustible insulation will be required for any fire separation.

Such details need to be carefully considered before work starts. Over-rafter insulation also takes time and it is usually advisable to fit a scaffold and temporary roof to safeguard the structure beneath. This comes with additional cost.

Wood fibreboards – over rafters (breathable)

Interlocking wood fibreboards have low thermal conductivity, high vapour-permeability and good airtightness and thermal mass, making them ideal for attic spaces. They also have far better acoustic insulation than foil-faced foam boards or quilts, an important factor if the house is on a road or in a noisy environment. Wood fibreboards specifically designed for over-rafter installation have a small amount of inert waterproofing additive (latex), so they can repel any moisture that breaches the tiles without the use of a membrane. They can be laid directly over rafters, and are then counter-battened and

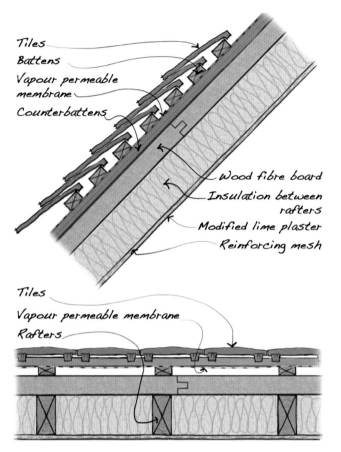

Tiles
Battens
Vapour permeable membrane
Counterbattens

Wood fibre board
Insulation between rafters
Modified lime plaster
Reinforcing mesh

Tiles
Vapour permeable membrane
Rafters

Left: Wood fibreboard over rafters. Technically this is the best place for the insulation but the roofline will be raised, affecting various external details.

Below: Wood fibre batts are first laid between rafters (below), followed by tongue-and-groove wood fibreboards fitted over the top to ensure an airtight layer (bottom).

battened before the tiles or slates are fixed, creating an all-important ventilation gap. Although they are ideal for a roof that is relatively straight, they are difficult to fix to an undulating roof due to their rigid structure.

Always choose a wood fibreboard with an interlocking edge. This will achieve much better airtightness than a butted edge and will improve both thermal and acoustic insulation. When used on roofs, the boards alone cannot achieve an adequate U-value so an insulation quilt or batt is added between the rafters.

Multi-foil insulation – over rafters (variable breathability)

One possible solution which minimises the thickness of over-rafter insulation is a multi-foil membrane. This combines thin layers of foam insulation and wadding, sandwiched between reflective foil layers and metallic film, and comes as a roll. It is a potential solution on an undulating roof where the top sides of the rafters are not in a flat plane.

Certain types of multi-foil insulation have a thickness of just 30mm, and claim to achieve the equivalent U-value of 210mm of mineral wool quilt. There has been scepticism over this claim and many building professionals remain unconvinced.

In order for multi-foil insulation to stand a chance of working, it must be very carefully installed, exactly to the manufacturer's instructions. The foil is laid directly over the rafters and pulled taut, then carefully taped at any junctions, to achieve good airtightness. Any untaped junction will result in a draught passing through, allowing cool air under the multi-foil and completely negating the value of the insulation.

If using a vapour-permeable roofing membrane above the insulation, a clear gap of 25mm is necessary between the membrane and the foil. This can be achieved with a standard-thickness roofing batten. The roofing membrane also has to be pulled taut so it does not sag and touch the multi-foil. This in itself may cause problems.

Anecdotal evidence suggests that properly installed multi-foil insulation is extremely effective. But the consequences of poor fitting will result in an ineffective insulation layer that cannot be accessed once the roof has been finished. Junctions around chimney stacks, ridges and eaves require particular attention, as gaps will allow draughts. In addition, there is the problem of lack

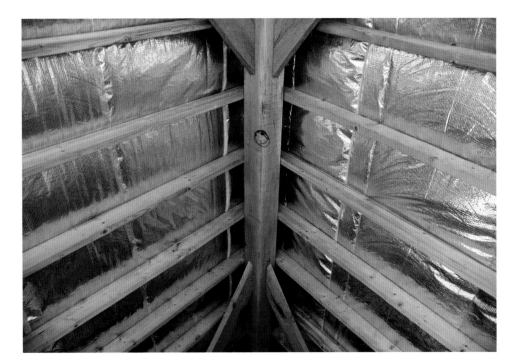

of breathability which may or may not be an issue. Various multi-foil products are advertised as being breathable, although the degree of breathability is sometimes disputed.

Only time will tell whether multi-foil insulation and the critical taped junctions have a lifespan to match a well-tiled roof, which can easily be from 50 to 75 years.

Rafter-level insulation from below

Where insulation is being added to the underside of the rafters without disturbing the tiles or slates, any solution should consider the following:

> What is the condition of the roof covering? Before attempting any insulation to the underside, replace any broken tiles or slates and address all defects.
> Is there an old lath and lime plaster ceiling fixed to the underside of the rafters? If the condition is good, an alternative solution should ideally be found that does not involve removing it.
> If you have a modern sloping ceiling, ascertain what it is made from. Is it modern plasterboard or fibreboard? If it is either of these, it should be relatively easy to take down and expose the rafters. CAUTION: if you have any concerns that it may be asbestos, it must be removed by a specialist firm.
> What condition are the rafters in? If they have been badly affected by beetle, or have rotted, it is important to repair them before covering them up,

Above: Correct installation is critical when using a multifoil insulation.

Below: This pantile roof in Norfolk does not need replacing, but its undulating structure will limit the options for insulation from below.

especially if you are applying more load to them with the weight of the insulation. This can usually be done quite easily by fixing extra timbers to the side of the existing rafters.

> Is there roofing felt above the rafters and under the tiles or slates? Is it the standard black bituminous type? If so, additional ventilation may be required.
> Do you need to incorporate vents within the tile/slate covering to prevent condensation forming on the underside?
> Has your roof deflected? Hold a straight edge horizontally along the underside of the rafters to assess how flat it is. While Victorian terraces are usually fairly straight, an older cottage constructed of undersized timbers or 'pole' rafters may be extremely bowed. Deflection frequently occurs in roofs that have had their original roof covering changed, for instance from thatch to clay tile which is heavier. A bowing roof structure will require an insulation product that can follow the shape of the roof, thus limiting the choice of products. If in any doubt, seek professional advice to check whether the roof is structurally sound.
> Do you need acoustic insulation? If so, a higher-density product should be sought, such as wood fibreboard.

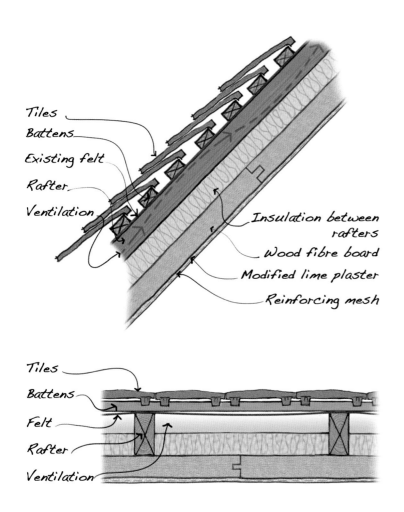

Tiles
Battens
Existing felt
Rafter
Ventilation

Insulation between rafters
Wood fibre board
Modified lime plaster
Reinforcing mesh

Tiles
Battens
Felt
Rafter
Ventilation

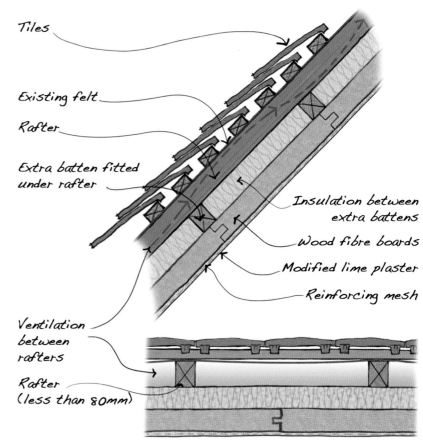

Tiles
Existing felt
Rafter
Extra batten fitted under rafter

Insulation between extra battens
Wood fibre boards
Modified lime plaster
Reinforcing mesh

Ventilation between rafters
Rafter (less than 80mm)

Wood fibreboard – under rafter (breathable)

For a relatively straight roof, wood fibreboard, combined with a breathable insulation quilt, is an ideal solution. If properly installed this provides sound insulation, and can be designed to prevent condensation.

It is important to leave a minimum of 50mm ventilated cavity above the insulation. If your rafters are less than 80mm deep, there is not enough depth for a quilt and an air gap. To create extra depth, it may be possible to fix extra battens under the rafters running at right angles to them. These should be the same depth as the proposed insulation quilt, which can be laid between them. The original rafters can then be left clear for ventilation.

Above left: Wood fibreboard under deep rafters. If the roof covering is sound and not due to be replaced for some years, wood fibreboard can be fixed under the rafters.

Above: Wood fibreboard under shallow rafters. If your rafters are less than 80mm deep, it will be necessary to fix extra battens under them, running at right angles to them, to accommodate the thickness of quilt, leaving the space between the rafters clear for ventilation (see photographic sequence on the following page).

1. The existing roof to this cottage consisted of thin-section oak rafters with 1970s impermeable roofing felt over. The roof space was to be converted to a habitable room, but as the tiles above were sound, the insulation was added from below.

2. Extra battens are fixed, at right angles to the underside of the narrow rafters, with the same width spacing as the insulation batt. Wood strips, as previously described, are also fitted to increase ventilation and reduce the condensation risk.

3. The insulation quilt is placed to fit snugly between the extra battens.

4. Tongue-and-groove wood fibreboard is fitted over the top and taped at any butted junctions.

5. The surface is skimmed with a base coat of modified lime plaster.

6. The plaster is keyed with a metal comb.

7. Fine mesh is gently pushed into the plaster to prevent cracking, minimising water vapour passing through. Once dry, a lime setting coat is applied on top.

8. The finished attic room. Note the purlins have been left exposed as they are set below the rafter line, but these could potentially act as a thermal bridge.

Foil faced foam board between rafters

Insulated plasterboard

Taped junctions and gypsum skim

Tile

Batten

Existing felt

50mm Ventilation air gap

Above: Foam board between and under rafters.

Right: This roof is being fitted with foam board between the rafters. Such insulation can also be added from below, but care should always be taken to minimise gaps and prevent condensation.

Foil-faced foam board and plasterboard – under rafter (non-breathable)

For a standard solution, which is familiar to most builders, modern foil-faced foam board can be fitted between the rafters in certain circumstances. This must fit tightly with minimal gaps at the edges. A further sheet of foam board is fixed under the rafters and is taped at the junctions to minimise moisture vapour passing through. This is finished with plasterboard (ideally foil-backed) and skim. Alternatively, insulated plasterboard can be fitted directly under the rafters.

This solution relies on an airtight barrier being formed, otherwise moisture vapour may penetrate and cause condensation on the underside of the felt. Make sure your builder is properly supervised and takes care to seal all junctions. Adequate ventilation is also critical to disperse any moisture under the felt.

> The rafter line needs to be relatively straight for this option as the boards cannot flex to fit.
> The thickness of boards used between the rafters will depend on their depth – remember to leave a 50mm gap between the top of the insulation and the underside of the felt. If the foam board fitted to the underside of the rafters is more than 50mm it may be difficult to fix the plasterboard because of the length of fixings required.
> Where foam board is only fitted between rafters (and not to the underside as well) a separate vapour barrier will need to be installed to provide airtightness.
> Avoid recessed light fittings as these will require holes to be cut through the plasterboard and insulation, allowing leakage of warm moist air into the roof structure above.
> While foil-faced foam board provides good thermal insulation, it has poor acoustic insulation compared to wood fibreboard.

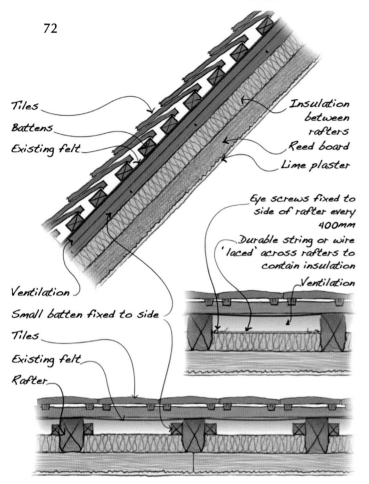

Tiles
Battens
Existing felt

Insulation between rafters
Reed board
Lime plaster

Eye screws fixed to side of rafter every 400mm
Durable string or wire 'laced' across rafters to contain insulation
Ventilation

Ventilation
Small batten fixed to side
Tiles
Existing felt
Rafter

Left: Reed board, fixed under the rafters, is a good solution for undulating roof structures. Consideration should be given to stopping the quilt pushing through and touching the underside of the felt. Where it is not practical to fit battens, metal eyelets can be screwed into the rafter sides at regular intervals and string can be laced across.

Getting the right contractor

The more complex the system of insulation, the more critical the workmanship becomes. It is crucial to appoint a contractor who understands the importance of airtightness and the dangers of thermal bridging, and who is familiar with the materials being used. Great care needs to be taken when installing the system, and ideally it should be thoroughly checked before it is covered over. A contractor who is working to a fixed price may rush the job or hand it over to a less skilled tradesman.

Quilt and reed matting or board – under rafter (breathable)

For undulating roof structures, where a rigid board system cannot flex to fit, a reed board may be an option, particularly where a traditional lime-plastered ceiling is desired. First a quilt is cut to shape and fitted between the rafters; ideally this should be a natural quilt with a 50mm ventilated gap above. Battens can be fixed to the side of the rafters to stop the insulation pushing through. A reed board (typically 20–50mm thick) is fixed to the underside of the rafters using stainless steel screws, giving additional insulation. This forms a good substrate for lime or clay plaster, which should be decorated with a breathable paint. This solution will not meet current U-values but it will improve the insulation to a ceiling where options are limited. Where rafters are less than 80mm deep, it may be impossible to fit a quilt and leave an adequate air gap. An extra batten can be fitted to the underside of the rafter to increase its thickness, or the thickest available reed board may be used without insulation quilt. This can be coated with up to 50mm of insulating lime plaster (➡ Insulating lime plasters, page 115). While not achieving a particularly good U-value, it will still be a marked improvement on the previous situation.

Above: Damaged lath and plaster on a sloped ceiling.

Right: The lath and plaster ceiling to this slope was in poor condition and carefully taken down. Due to the undulations in the rafters, 50mm reed board was fixed to the underside, and finished with two coats of insulating lime plaster. This may be a good solution for coombed ceilings with short slopes.

Spray foam insulation

Unfortunately, the practice of spraying foam on the underside of a roof has for many years been heralded as a perfect solution for old buildings. The technique uses expanding polyurethane foam, sprayed between the rafters, either to the underside of the roofing felt or, where there is no felt, directly to the tiles. It is advertised as a quick, cheap and easy solution to repair leaking and failing roofs.

Unfortunately, the reality is that it forms a very short stopgap and may well cause problems in the longer term. The impermeable foam covers parts of the rafters, potentially trapping dampness and causing their moisture content to rise, making them susceptible to beetle attack and decay. In addition, where spray foam is stuck to the underside of tiles or slates, it inhibits any future internal inspection of the roof for maintenance purposes and complicates minor repairs. It also prevents tiles and slates from being reused without great effort and expense in the future when the roof is next re-covered.

Left: Spray foam to the underside of a roof.

INSULATING DORMER WINDOWS

Dormer windows are notoriously difficult to insulate and are a common cause of thermal bridging in roofs. The 'cheeks' or triangular side walls to dormers are usually very thin. If they are built of timber studs, they will contain a cavity, often no more than 50mm. The rafters are also generally thin-section as they carry a limited load. Such narrow cavities minimise the opportunity for insulation but they should be insulated with quilt or foil-faced foam board. Be sure to get the insulation right into the corners, leaving no air voids. If possible, fit foam board or wood fibreboard over the rafters and under the slates or tiles. Insulation board can also be fixed on the outside of the cheeks with a suitable covering; a 20mm board will make a difference to insulation. The disadvantage to this is that it will raise the roof line and the width of the dormer and all the roof slates or tiles will have to be modified accordingly. Aerogel or multi-foil may be an option to avoid this.

THATCH AND INSULATION

Until recently, it was assumed that thatched roofs are in themselves excellent insulators and require no additional measures to improve their energy-efficiency. While this assumption remains true for many thatched roofs, in certain cases thatch may require a helping hand. Due to its organic nature, thatch needs to breathe or it will rot. Inappropriate alterations that raise the moisture content by preventing the thatch from drying out will considerably shorten its life.

The U-value of thatch is dependent on a number of variables:

> Thickness: the thicker the thatch, the better the insulation. Long straw and combed wheat reed are generally built up in layers over many centuries and are often up to 1m thick. Conversely, water reed is stripped to the rafters and applied in a single 300mm coat.

> Pitch: a steeper roof will shed water more quickly and retain less moisture. The drier the thatch, the better insulator it will be.

> Condition: a well-maintained thatch will perform better than one in poor condition. If not maintained, abutment details around chimney stacks and dormers can let in draughts while vermin and bird holes also reduce thermal efficiency.

Recent tests have established that 300mm water reed can achieve an average U-value of $0.29W/m^2K$, and 300mm long straw approximately $0.23W/m^2K$. Combed wheat reed falls somewhere between these two figures. As the latter two types are often laid in much thicker layers, their U-value is likely to meet, or come close to, Building Regulations.

The main problem with thatch tends not to be in its U-value and its effectiveness as an insulator, but with draughts and air infiltration. Water reed in particular tends to lack airtightness due to its structure and application. All thatch types can be particularly draughty at junctions and abutments, and particularly at the eaves where draughts are commonplace. This negates some of the thermal effectiveness of the thatch.

If thatched roof spaces are not occupied (cold roofs), the best solution is to insulate the flat ceilings to the rooms below as already described. To maximise the life of the thatch, encourage ventilation to the underside by clearing the eaves and getting a good through draught.

If the roof space is occupied (warm roof), an airtight-

Top: Thatched roofs can provide excellent insulation.

Above: Thatch in poor condition will hold more moisture and be thermally less efficient.

ness test ( Airtightness test, page 42) will quickly establish how much draught is entering the room and from where. Vapour-permeable materials such as lime mortar and tightly compacted natural quilts can be used to plug draughts. These will wick water away rather than hold it against the thatch. It is important not to use impermeable materials next to thatch as these will trap moisture at the interface and accelerate decay. A thermal imaging test will highlight any areas of thermal bridging, for instance where tile has been used in conjunction with thatch but not properly insulated beneath.

When applying a ceiling to the sloping underside of a thatched roof, it is important to use a breathable solution, particularly where draughts have been minimised and ventilation to the underside no longer exists. Depending on the condition of the thatch, this can be done by plastering with lime or clay directly to the underside, between the rafters, and leaving the timber structure exposed. If historic smoke-blackened thatch exists, a different solution would have to be considered. Given the complexities and costs of thatching, always consult a specialist if altering traditional details.

Above: 300-year-old clay plaster applied directly to the underside of the original basecoat of thatch. A rare survival, it has a beautiful texture and was carefully repaired when the house was brought back into use. Note the 'pole' rafters, probably in softwood, which are particularly vulnerable to decay if exposed to damp for a prolonged period.

FLAT ROOFS

Traditionally, flat roofs were formed over joists and were laid with what were essentially plain-edged floorboards with small gaps in between to accommodate seasonal movement and aid ventilation. Over this deck, lead, copper, zinc and other metals were commonly laid.

From the mid-twentieth century onwards, flat-roofed extensions have been a common feature of old buildings as a cheap way of adding extra space. Modern flat roofs, or old roofs that have been repaired or upgraded, are likely to have a more modern deck of wooden sheet materials such as chipboard or ply, and might incorporate an underlay. This may be covered with traditional materials, mastic asphalt or more recently developed roofing products such as synthetic membranes. Internally there is likely to be a ceiling, either of plasterboard or lath and plaster.

The two key points to remember are that 'flat' roofs should generally never be totally flat, as they need to shed water, and that the materials used on them must allow for contraction and expansion to cope with changes in temperature resulting from the weather.

Adding insulation

As with all types of roof, the main concern when adding thermal insulation is ensuring condensation does not form within the roof structure. There are a variety of ways of insulating a flat roof. The insulation may be:

> fitted beneath the roof structure just above the ceiling, leaving the structure ventilated and colder than the room below to create a 'cold deck'

> installed above the roof structure but beneath the waterproof covering, maintaining the temperature of the structure close to that of the room below to form a 'warm deck'

> laid above the waterproof covering, but beneath a protective layer such as screed, soil or pebbles as an 'inverted deck'

> fixed within the living space below the ceiling

Gaining access to install insulation in flat roofs is generally difficult except when either the roof covering or the ceiling below is being renewed. Not all flat roofs are deep enough to accommodate the thickness of insulation required along with the necessary ventilation space, so it will either be necessary to compromise on the level of insulation provided or to deepen the overall build-up of the roof. This can present aesthetic and practical difficulties and is especially problematic where pitched and other roofs run into the flat roof. In all cases it is essential that the roof has a sufficient fall to ensure water is shed and that any flashing around its perimeter is of sufficient depth to be effective.

Windows and doors

Few building elements have a greater aesthetic impact than windows and doors. Sadly, they are frequently the first items to be replaced, often in the name of energy-efficiency. Time and again this work is ill-conceived and unnecessary, the results devaluing the building and destroying the special qualities that set it apart.

Draughty windows and doors are often regarded as just a fact of life. This need not be the case; sensitive upgrading and repair can be straightforward and hugely effective in the battle against heat loss.

Windows and doors contribute much to the historic integrity of a building and are frequently important in maintaining the look of a whole street. Simple measures are a good investment since they will achieve energy savings while causing the minimum loss of historic character, helping to protect the value of your house over the longer term.

The replacement of original windows and doors has more than high monetary and aesthetic costs. It means that all the embodied energy and carbon within them is lost and valuable resources have to be used to make the replacements. It is worth remembering that, historically, the timber used in joinery was usually slow-grown, more durable and of far better quality than is generally available today.

Replacing a window not only results in the loss of the frame but of the latches and other fittings. Just as important is the glass. Old handmade glass has ripples, air bubbles and other manufacturing 'defects' that add

sparkle to the face of a building. In comparison, modern machine-made glass is flat and lifeless.

BUILDING REGULATIONS

Under the Building Regulations, windows and doors within their frames are referred to as 'controlled fittings'. In existing buildings, controlled fittings need to be upgraded to comply with current U-values under the circumstances listed in Chapter 2, page 29. More specifically, when a controlled fitting is replaced, compliance is also required. However, replacing a window or door while retaining the existing frame does not constitute a controlled fitting, and therefore does not have to comply.

The Building Regulations recognise the need to protect traditional and historic facades to old buildings, and therefore may accept a lower centre-pane U-value

Opposite: Doors and windows are the face of a building.

Below: Original doors and windows give old buildings charm and character and are valuable assets that are worth retaining.

Left: Many old windows have special exemptions from Building Regulations.

Below left: Thermal images of an old sash window before and after secondary glazing was added.

Preserving value

Windows are recognised as being valuable assets. In a survey by English Heritage, 82 per cent of estate agents felt that original features such as sash windows tend to add financial value to properties, while 78 per cent believed they help to sell a property more quickly.

Below: Traditional doors, windows and shutters in Spitalfields, London.

for individual replacement windows that need to match existing ones. They may also accept single glazing supplemented with Low-E secondary glazing (➡ page 90).

OLD WINDOWS ARE EFFICIENT

Testing has revealed that a typical historic window has an overall U-value of between 4.4 and 4.8 W/m²K. This is dependent on the style of the window and the proportion of glass to wood.

When we compare this to the U-value targets in the 2010 Building Regulations, stating that a window must meet 2.0 W/m²K, we can immediately see the inefficiency of single glazing. A typical double-glazed window has a U-value of 1.9W/m²K.

Research has proved, however, that with care and sensitive intervention traditional windows can perform better than double glazing. The research looked at various options for reducing heat loss through a traditional sash window, without resorting to replacement. The results showed overwhelmingly how simple measures can improve the energy-efficiency of old windows and bring them into line with current U-value requirements.

U-value test results

Glasgow Caledonian University carried out a series of 'hot box' tests on an old sash window that had been repaired. First they established the U-value of the window in its existing form, then they calculated the improved thermal efficiency following a variety of simple measures.

	Whole window U-value	Heat loss reduction
Victorian sash window, 2 over 2 panes	4.3	—
Heavy curtains	2.5	42%
Traditional, well-fitting shutters	1.7	60%
Plain roller blind	2.7	37%
Reflective roller blind	1.9	56%
Insulated honeycomb blind	2.1	51%
Low-E secondary glazing	1.8	58%
Low-E secondary glazing and shutters	1.6	63%

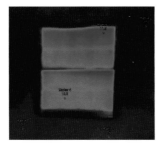

Left: Heat flux monitor on a single-glazed window pane.

REPAIR OR REPLACE?

Owners of old houses are constantly under pressure to upgrade leaky windows and doors. Targeted marketing from window renewal companies frequently promises instant energy-efficiency, maintenance-free plastics and cost-saving special offers. Unsurprisingly, many people have been seduced by the 'quick fix' of PVCu – polyvinyl chloride un-plasticised, also known as uPVC.

At their worst, these plastic windows look heavy and out of proportion but manufacturers are now producing ranges of plastic mouldings far more akin to their wooden forebears. So is there ever a case for replacing traditional windows with quality PVCu lookalikes?

A product of the petrochemical industry, PVCu is a material that is toxic and energy-hungry in its production and non-biodegradable when scrapped. Despite the availability of recycling schemes, these windows frequently end up in landfill. Sadly, plastic windows have often replaced perfectly good wooden windows which could easily have been overhauled and upgraded to make them considerably more energy-efficient.

In the eighteenth and nineteenth centuries, Baltic pine was imported to make many of the windows that survive today. This was slow-grown, straight-grained and particularly durable. It is not uncommon to find wooden windows that are 100, 200 or even 300 years old and still in good condition. If they are damaged, a good local joiner or one of the many companies that specialise in this work should be able to make relatively inexpensive repairs, something that is virtually impossible to do with plastic windows as the whole unit generally has to be replaced.

A reputable firm can make a high-quality wood window from sustainably sourced timber with an expected life span of at least 60 years. High-performance timber windows need be no more expensive than their PVCu equivalents: research into lifetime costs has shown that wood windows work out 2–7 per cent cheaper than PVCu.

Above: These early nineteenth-century windows in Oxfordshire were carefully repaired and draughtproofed.

Above: Replacement PVCu windows (on the left) can spoil and devalue an old house unnecessarily.

FIRST THINGS FIRST

There are numerous ways of upgrading old windows that are often cheaper and more energy-efficient than whole-sale replacement. Before doing anything, ask yourself these questions so you can make an informed choice on treatment:

> ### How frequently does the window get opened?

For instance, a window on a roadside elevation may remain permanently closed. If this is the case, a single panel of glass or plastic discreetly fixed, but designed to lift out to facilitate cleaning, may be the ideal option.

> ### Is it important to improve security to the window?

Ground-floor windows on the street side can be particularly vulnerable. Any upgrading may need to incorporate security measures.

> ### Do you open the window in the warmer months but keep it closed in winter?

Many windows will come into this category. If so, temporary, fixed-pane secondary glazing, which is easy to put up in the winter but can be taken down and stored in the spring, could be the perfect solution.

> ### Do you open the window on a regular basis throughout the year?

Bathroom windows in particular come into this category. Carefully considered and properly installed extractor fans can reduce the need for open windows in steamy rooms.

> ### Are you looking for good acoustic performance from your window?

Houses in the flight path of an airport or near a busy road will need special consideration to minimise noise pollution. Secondary glazing is particularly successful in this instance, and performs far better than double glazing.

> ### Does the window form part of an emergency escape route?

If so, secondary glazing is usually unsuitable as it will increase the time required to open it and may restrict the size of the opening.

CURTAINS, BLINDS AND SHUTTERS

Before tackling the windows themselves, think about the other options available. Curtains and shutters have long been used to reduce both heat loss and heat gain and it is worth looking at ways of improving their thermal performance.

Heavy insulated curtains

It might sound obvious, but a heavy curtain is a simple way of reducing the heat loss through a single-glazed window.

There are a number of things to consider if designing a curtain for this purpose:
> Fit the curtain from floor to ceiling where possible, otherwise the cool air between the curtain and the glass will flow out of the bottom and create a draught.
> Hem the curtains in-situ and make sure they are touching the floor. Even a small gap of a few

Left: Hanging heavy insulated curtains will significantly reduce heat loss.

Above: A specially designed 'thermal blind'.

Thermal blinds

Various ranges of insulated blinds are available that will assist in reducing heat loss through old windows, sometimes even more successfully than curtains. The blinds incorporate a variety of insulating and reflective layers designed to minimise conductivity through the fabric. These are carefully fitted to create a 'seal' around the edge of the blind, usually by screwing a lightweight metal runner to the window frame. Some systems incorporate magnets, which hold the blind against the frame. Always discuss your particular window with the blind manufacturer to check compatibility before ordering.

Shutters

Wood is a good insulator so, as long as they are well fitted, shutters can dramatically reduce heat loss. Consider overhauling existing shutters, provided there will not be an unacceptable level of alteration and loss of historic character. They must fit tightly, meeting with a rebated edge rather than a square butt joint, ideally with some sort of brush strip or rubber seal.

The disadvantage of standard shutters is that they only work at night so do not assist with energy-efficiency during daylight hours when the shutters are open. Where your window reveal is splayed or designed to take a shutter but the original is missing, a glazed shutter may be an ideal solution. This is a bespoke piece of joinery which contains a double glazed unit within a frame, rather than a wooden panel. It can be permanently closed in the winter months, allowing daylight to pass through while keeping out draughts, and folded back out of the way in the warmer months when the window is regularly opened.

millimetres at the base of the curtains will allow the leakage of cool air.

> If you have a radiator under a window that cannot be relocated, fit a shelf above the radiator for the curtain to 'sit' on, preventing warm air rising behind the curtain and disappearing through the window.

> While not appropriate for every window, a pelmet to the top of the curtain helps to close off draughts and stop warm air disappearing down the back.

> Set the curtain pole or rail as close to the wall as possible. This is often difficult to achieve as brackets are frequently designed to set the pole a couple of inches proud of the wall, in which case they may need adapting. A big gap at the top or the side will dramatically reduce the benefit of the curtains. Alternatively, close the gap with a board down the side of the window, designed to appear as part of the frame. These measures will all help create an 'airlock' between curtain and window.

> The curtains should be lined with an insulating lining and interlined with heavy fleece; both are available as standard from curtain manufacturers and high-street stores. Buy the best quality you can afford.

> Bear in mind that these curtains are heavier than standard so any curtain track or pole should be fitted with this in mind.

Right: Well-fitting shutters are a good way of retaining heat at night.

Far right: Glazed shutters can be kept shut while allowing the light in during the day.

DRAUGHTPROOFING

Draughtproofing is a means of reducing the gap between the window casement or the sash and the frame. Carefully executed, this is an ideal solution where a window is regularly opened, and is virtually invisible when the window is closed. There are two main types of draughtproofing seals: compression seals and wiper seals.

Selecting the right seal

Specialist draughtproofing companies tend to carry a standard product, and joiners may have a preferred choice of seal, but there are many new products on the market that are worth researching. Speak to a variety of manufacturers; most have a technical adviser to answer specific queries. Ask for a sample before placing a large order and check it is compatible with your situation. Buy the best-quality seals you can afford.

Above: A simple leather strip, fixed to the window frame with copper nails, is an early solution to draughtproofing.

Below: Professional draughtproofing involves cutting a rebate around sashes or casements. Ensure that a qualified person is employed to carry out the work.

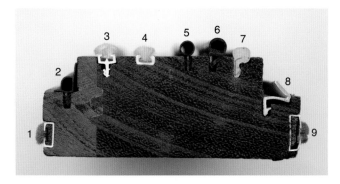

Above: Samples of various draughtproofing products.
1, 4, 9: Different colours and sizes of brush pile seals in self-adhesive pile carrier.
2: 'Bubble' compression seal for internal corners of frames.
3: Brush pile seal in push-fit pile carrier.
5, 6: Small and large push-fit 'bubble' seals.
7: Foam or 'cushion' compression seal with HDPE skin.
8: 'V'-section push-fit compression seal or 'spring seal'.

> **Compression seals** are designed for use on hinged windows where the casement closes against the frame and the seal compresses to fill the gap. They come in various forms, usually made from EDPM rubber or silicone, or are made of foam, coated in a tough polymer skin of HDPE that sheds any paint that comes into contact with it.

> **Wiper seals** are generally used in sliding applications, for instance on the meeting rails of sash windows where the upper sash slides across the lower sash. These are usually a brush pile, held in a plastic carrier and rebated into position.

> **Brush pile seals** can also be used as compression seals but tend to lose their springiness over time, squashing down and failing to fill the gap.

Above: Draughtproofing in progress.

Stick-on solutions

Surface-mounted self-adhesive draughtproofing strips tend to fail fairly quickly. Even where the adhesive is strong, the painted surface on to which they are glued is often lumpy or flaky so a strong bond is rarely achieved. Certain rubber compression seals become slightly sticky in warm weather so adhere to the face of the door or window and get pulled off the frame on which they are mounted. This is particularly problematic on south-facing elevations. While surface-mounted strips are always better than nothing, for a long-lasting solution choose seals that are either fixed with pins or screws, or rebated into position.

Draughtproofing checklist

Check the firm is reputable and the joiners are experienced.

> Ask about the quality of the brush strips/compression seals and request a sample – some cheaper versions will compress very quickly and fail to keep out the draughts after a short time.

> Seals and brush strips are usually available in white and black so choose the best match for your window.

> If painting windows after they have been draughtproofed, avoid getting paint on the seals as this may stop them working effectively.

> On sash windows, ensure any replacement 'staff beads' and 'parting beads' are wood and not plastic.

> Draughtproofing companies will often plane the edges of sashes or casements so ensure they are painted with a primer before they are put back in the frames, otherwise they will swell and jam. Most firms do not allocate time to allow primers to dry, hence they do not bother – ask about this in advance.

> When the window is re-assembled, ensure the window furniture is working correctly so it can be closed tightly.

> If you are replacing sash fasteners, choose a good quality 'cam action' fastener. These push the sashes tightly against the top and bottom seals, as well as pulling them together to create a good airtight seal.

> A properly draughtproofed window should open and close smoothly, and not rattle. If it rattles, it is likely to have gaps and draughts.

Draughtproofing should be top of the agenda when upgrading old windows. But it is only partially effective when trying to achieve energy-efficiency: it only deals with heat loss via draughts, and does not address conductivity of heat through the glass itself.

Draughtproofing metal windows

Modern metal windows, usually post-1965, tend to have weatherstrips set in either preformed grooves or factory-fixed channels. Older metal windows pose a particular problem when it comes to draughtproofing as seals cannot be set into the frame or mechanically fixed.

Above: Arts and Crafts metal window.

Gaps around opening windows can be minimised either by a specialist firm employing a patented liquid silicone draughtproofing system or by a dextrous homeowner, ideally following redecoration. The basic technique is:

> Open any hinged windows.
> Ensure surfaces are clean, dry and free from dust.
> Apply a low-tack tape or release agent to the closing edges of the window casement where it touches the frame when closed.
> Using a mastic gun, apply a bead of silicone to the closing edge of the frame – use either a matching colour or clear silicone.
> Close the windows immediately after applying the silicone – this will cause it to squash out and be moulded to the shape of the gap.
> Allow 48 hours for it to cure. Do not open the window during this time.
> Once dry, open the window and remove the low-tack tape. The silicone should be adhered to the frame rather than the opening window.
> Trim back the silicone to produce a tidy finish.

Left: Leaded lights tend to be draughty due to their poor fit.

SECONDARY GLAZING

Secondary glazing comes in a variety of forms, either in glass or plastic, and can be a good option for draughty windows. It is far more discreet than it used to be and, with careful planning, may almost disappear from view.

The big advantage of secondary glazing over draughtproofing is that it not only dramatically improves airtightness but also reduces heat loss via conductivity through the glass. This can make a great difference to the U-value of a single-glazed window. For maximum thermal performance, a Low-E glass should be specified. A well-fitted secondary system is acoustically superior to double glazing and can easily cut down noise through the window by over 50 per cent. This is a great bonus for anyone living on a busy road.

Secondary glazing tends to work best on windows that are never opened, or windows that are permanently closed during the winter months. If either of these situations apply, a single panel, set on a magnetic strip, can be used. Even if the window is kept shut, the secondary glazing will still need to be lifted out twice a year for the cavity to be cleaned.

Where panels are removed during the warmer summer months, they may be stored under a bed. The magnetic tape which is fixed to the window frame can be painted the same colour as the woodwork to disguise it while the panel is out.

There is a temptation to combine secondary glazing with draughtproofing. Recent advice suggests that, unless the secondary glazing is totally airtight, the original window should not be draughtproofed. This will help to ventilate the cavity and disperse any steaming up caused by interstitial condensation.

Below: Toughened glass lift-out panel on a magnetic strip.

Secondary glazing – glass

Various companies now specialise in glass secondary glazing for old buildings. This can be made to bespoke shapes and sizes, tailored to fit the most out-of-square windows and almost any opening. Such units have to be measured individually and usually come as toughened glass. This process adds considerable cost to the finished unit but is a good permanent solution. Toughened glass is also ideal for windows that are low down, particularly where young children use the room.

Units can now be made with slim-profile aluminium frames, powder-coated to match your internal paint scheme. If you are opting for a colour other than white, make sure that the rubber seal where the glass meets the aluminium trim is also colour-matched, rather than white or black. Better-quality secondary glazing incorporates Low-E glass, improving energy-efficiency.

This solution works best with single, lift-out panels that are not designed to be opened. Remember that the bigger the window, the heavier and more unwieldy it becomes, making lifting out more difficult; any panel over one metre square generally requires two people to lift it for maintenance purposes.

Secondary glazing can also be designed as sliding panels to access opening windows, although the benefits are not quite as great. These have to be fixed to the frame, and are therefore not designed to be removed during the warmer months, or lifted out for redecorating. Ask the manufacturer about these issues as some designs make it notoriously difficult to access the cavity for maintenance.

Openable secondary glazed panels are usually mounted on a sliding track which is thicker than the trim used for a fixed panel. Depending on the design, there will usually be a bar across the middle of the window (either horizontal or vertical) to divide the sliding panels. While these are still much slimmer, and therefore less obtrusive than they used to be, they are more visible

Leaded lights

Leaded lights can be notoriously cold and draughty for a number of reasons:

> gaps around the individual 'quarries' (the tiny panes of glass) reduce airtightness
> leaded panels are often set in metal frames which are poorly fitted and allow draughts
> the lead 'cames' holding the panel together act as thermal bridges

Leaded lights in particularly poor condition may need repairing to address the major leaks. Lift-out secondary glazing is usually a good solution to improve the overall thermal performance.

Below: It is worth considering ways to draughtproof leaded lights.

Left: Sliding secondary glazing in closed (left) and open (right) positions.

Below: single-panel lift-out secondary glazing installed (left) and being lifted out (right).

Top tip: DIY window insulation

For a cheap and effective temporary solution, special transparent film, similar to cling film, can be fitted over windows. Usually fixed with double-sided tape, it pulls taut when heated with a hairdryer. This creates an air cavity to reduce heat loss, but it prevents the window being opened.

Left: Transparent film will dramatically improve a draughty window.

Right: Carefully installed, plastic panels with magnetic tape fixing can be discreet, and are often an ideal expedient during the cooler months.

than a fixed panel. Ensure the inner frames line up with the meeting rails or mullions of the original window.

For vertically sliding sash windows, a secondary glazed inner sash arrangement is installed. Smaller windows are not usually fitted with counterweights, and can be tricky to open. For larger windows, a hinged or counterbalanced design may be necessary due to the weight of the glass. The frames to such units are far thicker so visually they are not always acceptable. Ask to see a model before ordering as some designs are far superior to others. In particular, check the seals and ensure they fit well when closed.

Secondary glazing – plastic

This may initially sound like an unattractive option, but plastic secondary glazing has many advantages and can be even more discreet than glass. It is particularly good for large windows where a non-opening, lift-out panel is required and where glass would simply be too heavy to facilitate maintenance.

Sheets can be ordered cut to size, and supplied with a self-adhesive magnetic strip to stick around the edge. A metal self-adhesive strip is fitted to the window frame to hold the panel in place. The better-quality strips are foam-backed to accommodate any irregularities in the surface to which you are sticking it. If you measure the window and assemble the panel yourself, this type of glazing is much cheaper than glass.

If your window is out of square or an unusual shape, you will probably need a bespoke solution manufactured from a template taken from the window. To check whether the window is square, measure the two diagonals: if they vary slightly it is not, and the plastic sheet

Right: A self-adhesive magnetic strip is fitted around the edge of the panel.

Centre: A self-adhesive metal strip is fitted to the window frame.

Far right: The plastic panel is offered up to the window.

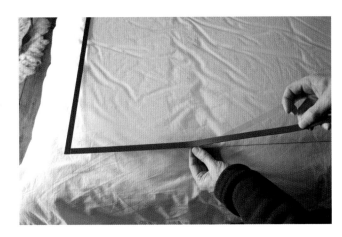

will need to be cut to suit. Depending on the type of plastic used, it may be possible to cut it with an ordinary jigsaw on-site. Woodworking planes can be used on most plastics to trim edges.

The advantages of plastic secondary glazing over glass are numerous:

> The better-quality plastics are completely clear and are indistinguishable from glass.
> They are much lighter in weight, and therefore easy to remove for cleaning or during summer.
> Because they are so lightweight, they do not require a trim or frame, as is the case with glass, and can be mounted on far more discreet magnetic strips, typically just 12.5mm wide, even for large panels.
> They are much cheaper than glass secondary glazing and can be assembled easily.

There are a number of considerations when fitting plastic secondary glazing:

> The plastic will pick up a static charge very easily and attract fluff, so avoid contact with carpets during assembly.
> Unlike glass, the sheets are extremely vulnerable to scratching. Keep them covered with their protective film as long as possible while fitting and take great care not to scratch them when cleaning. Scratch-resistant versions are available but these are very expensive.
> If storing during the warmer months, protect them with an old cotton duvet cover or pillow case.

Plastics for secondary glazing

Three principal plastics are used for secondary glazing:

> **Clear polystyrene** is the cheapest. It yellows over time and should only be used on the north elevation where it is not subjected to direct sunlight.
> **Cast acrylic** is the second cheapest. It contains a UV inhibitor and can therefore be used on any elevation. This is far more brittle, and requires specialist cutting equipment.
> **Polycarbonate** is the most expensive. It contains UV inhibitors but is also extremely tough (it is used for aircraft windscreens). This is a good option if you have low-level windows that could be a safety issue for children. It is also ideal for windows that require a security upgrade. If using polycarbonate for these reasons, additional fixing, in addition to the magnetic strip, will be required.

DOUBLE GLAZING

In simple terms, double glazing consists of two sheets of glass combined in a single unit, hermetically sealed around the edge with the space between filled with air, a vacuum or other gases. This reduces the transfer of both heat and noise through the unit. Units are typically between 24mm and 28mm thick and the seals create a border around the edge of at least 10mm. Modern windows are designed with these dimensions in mind, and have wide and deep rebates to accommodate the unit.

Warranties for double glazing vary enormously. A key issue is the problem of the seals failing and condensation forming within the unit. In an attempt to counter this, the spacers that hold the glass apart are filled with or contain desiccant. Even so, typical double-glazed units last between five and fifteen years before they steam up in the middle. Careful fitting and good window maintenance will increase the life of a double-glazed unit by preventing water from reaching the edge seals.

Most traditional windows have a glazing bar with a shallow rebate, designed to take a single sheet of hand-made glass, typically 3mm, and a thin fillet of linseed oil putty. This means it is usually impractical to replace old glass with standard 24mm-thick double-glazed units as there is insufficient width or depth. Where new windows are manufactured to take double-glazed units, the glazing bars are often oversized and out of proportion with the window.

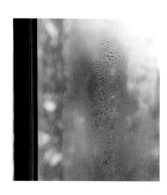

Left: A typical double-glazed window with a white spacer.

Right: A double-glazed unit that has failed and 'steamed up'.

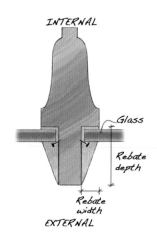
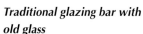
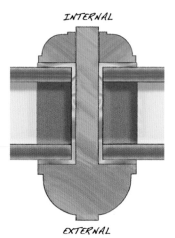
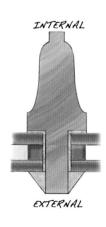

INTERNAL

Glass

Rebate depth

Rebate width

EXTERNAL

INTERNAL

EXTERNAL

INTERNAL

EXTERNAL

Traditional glazing bar with old glass

The size and proportions of traditional glazing bars varies enormously. Here the rebate is 15mm deep, allowing for a pane of 3mm handmade glass, secured by 'sprigs' (tiny nails) bedded in, and weatherproofed with a fillet of linseed oil putty. Some rebate depths may be as little as 12mm or less.

Modern glazing bar with standard unit

A modern double-glazed unit is typically 24mm to 28mm thick, with a wide visible border around the edge. Glazing bars to new windows are designed to fit the thicker units and to cover the border by having deeper and wider rebates. Most modern windows have internal wooden beads to secure the glazing units.

Traditional glazing bar with slim unit

A 10mm-thick slim-profile unit will fit some existing glazing bars but certainly not all. A rebate with a minimum depth of 18mm is necessary. The new unit is held in place with high-modulus clear silicone, without the need for 'sprigs'. This also makes the edge weathertight if properly applied, prolonging the life of the window. A small fillet of linseed oil putty finishes the glazing bar in the traditional manner, and should cover the border to the glazing unit.

Below: Slender traditional glazing bars in a single-glazed window.

Below: Chunky modern glazing bars for a double-glazed multi-pane window.

Slim-profile double-glazed units

In recent years a new generation of slim-profile double-glazed units has been developed, designed specifically for use in slender, traditionally sized glazing bars. Some are filled with low conductivity gases such as krypton and xenon and are able to meet current Building Regulations for U-values at just 12mm thick. They are also available as thin as 10mm, and some are manufactured with a narrow border or 'sightline' of 5mm. Where glazing bars are slender, a border wider than this may be visible. Some units can be ordered with an outer layer of handmade glass to suit a particular style and age of house.

In practical terms, few traditional glazing bars are deep enough to fit even a 10mm thick double-glazed panel. A minimum rebate depth of 18mm is required; this would allow an 8mm fillet of linseed oil putty to be applied.

An alternative is vacuum-filled units, available with a thickness of just over 6mm. While these sound like a good solution, they are manufactured with tiny spacers between the panes that appear as 'dots' on the glass which may be visually unacceptable.

Slim-profile double glazing allows new windows to be made to thermally efficient standards while retaining traditional proportions. It is also marketed to replace panes in existing windows as a way of reducing heat loss through the glass. Where old handmade glass is still present, however, this is inadvisable as it would spoil the character of the facade and the payback period would be so long that it would not be economically viable. Removal of handmade glass is unlikely to gain consent if a building is listed. Also bear in mind that the extra weight of a double-glazed unit may strain the hinges of casement windows and will almost certainly unbalance sashes.

As relatively new products, it is not yet clear how long slim-profile units will last before the seals fail and condensation forms in the middle. Importantly, double-glazing units should be set in a low-modulus silicone to prevent moisture reaching the edge seals. For the best quality, look for the longest possible guarantee and systems that meet all six of the relevant European standards and comply with BS EN 1279.

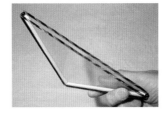

Above: Slim-profile double glazing.

Below: This PVCu window has been discarded after just a few years.

Bottom: A new, traditionally proportioned single-glazed wooden window being fitted.

REPLACING MODERN WINDOWS

A house with its original sashes will often fetch a premium over a neighbouring property where the windows have been replaced. Unsurprisingly, many homeowners are keen to take out PVCu or aluminium windows and reinstate something more in keeping with the period of the house.

What are the options?

Generally, when a window within its frame is replaced, the work is notifiable. This means that an application for Building Regulations consent should be made and the new unit should meet current U-values. The regulations accept that replacement windows in certain period properties cannot achieve the current U-values without severely compromising their design, and a relaxed value is accepted (see Building Regulations, page 29). If your house is listed, you may find that your conservation officer insists on single glazing.

Ideally, new windows in period facades should combine the appearance and proportion of the old windows with a reasonable level of energy-efficiency. Regardless of whether the building is listed, it may be possible to fit a facsimile, traditional window with single-glazed, handmade glass. This can be designed to work in conjunction with a secondary glazed unit which meets current U-values. This solution should satisfy building control and, where appropriate, the conservation officer.

Below: Spacers set within a double-glazed unit awaiting 'planted-on' glazing bars.

Top tip: Double-glazing spacer bars

Where double-glazed units are used, avoid aluminium or silver-coloured spacer bars which draw the eye. Instead, shop around for a spacer bar that is less visually obvious such as black, white or cream.

New windows fitted with slim-profile double glazing (see above) can achieve good U-values while allowing a traditional-section glazing bar to be incorporated in the design. For the best visual effect, the outer pane of glass can be specified as handmade, but with multi-pane windows consisting of many small panes this comes at a price. If the seals to the slim-profile double-glazed units fail, and the guarantee is no longer valid, it can become an expensive maintenance item.

A much cheaper solution is to use a single, standard-thickness, double-glazed unit with 'stick-on' or 'planted-on' glazing bars to create the appearance of a multi-pane window. This must be well done and, to give a more convincing effect close up, the glazed units can be fitted with spacers sandwiched between the two layers of glass to correspond with the stick-on glazing bars. This is of course a visual cheat, and will not provide the same aesthetic appeal as a traditionally constructed window, but it may still be preferable to a PVCu unit and be within a more modest budget than any of the alternatives. In their favour, windows with stick-on glazing bars have a superior U-value to the multi-pane solution outlined above, as a real glazing bar acts as a thermal bridge.

Low-E glass

Glass is now available with a Low-E coating, which reflects radiant infrared energy rather than allowing it to pass through. Windows can be designed to reflect heat back into the room, making them more energy-efficient during the winter, or to reflect solar gain, keeping the internal environment cool during the summer.

INTRODUCING EXTRA DAYLIGHT

Old buildings can have dark interiors, especially when internal layouts have been rearranged. Bringing in natural daylight will reduce the need for electric lighting but careful thought should be given to the introduction of new glazing.

Conservation rooflights

Modern rooflights tend to look incongruous in old buildings, as they stand proud of the slates or tiles. Far more acceptable are 'conservation rooflights' which are set flush with the pitch of the roof, and often incorporate a central glazing bar to imitate the early cast-iron versions. Many rooflight manufacturers sell a range of conservation rooflights, some of which are far better than others. Always ask to see a photograph of the rooflight fitted into an existing roof and compare the visual impact of each one. Measure the distance between your rafters and try to choose a rooflight that will fit in between, or at least have minimum impact on the historic roof structure.

Thermal bridging tends to be a problem with rooflights and condensation can occur. Ask the manufacturer about these issues and try to select a product that provides the best thermal specification.

Above: Rooflights can be fitted from the inside without the need for scaffolding.

Right: A barn conversion in Oxfordshire with specially designed glazing for extra light.

Below: Sun pipes are a good way of introducing light.

Sun pipes

Sun pipes or tubes are a way of bringing natural light into the heart of a building. In certain circumstances, they may be appropriate in old buildings, particularly on double-pitch roofs where they can be hidden in the central valley. While they perform well, it is important to consider their visual impact both at roof level and within the room where they emerge. Care needs to be taken to decide the exact route taken by the pipe to ensure that the minimum damage is caused to the fabric, especially where it is necessary to cut through joists or ceilings. As few roof tiles as possible should be removed to install the transparent external dome.

Routes from the top of the tube to the internal diffuser need to be kept as short and straight as possible: 10 per cent of usable light is lost at every bend. Smooth-sided tubes are said to offer superior performance. A south-facing roof is the optimum position for the dome and, if sited on a north face, it should be positioned as high as possible. When used in a prominent position, a conservation version is available with a flat top rather than a dome.

Top tip: Self-cleaning glass

If you are adding rooflights or glazing an area that is inaccessible, consider using self-cleaning glass. There are various types so check which is most suitable for your application.

Left: Self-cleaning glass is useful where windows are inaccessible, as in the case of this conservation rooflight.

Top: Georgian door and doorcase in Spitalfields, London.

Top right: A well-maintained door can last for many years.

Above: When working on old doors, take the opportunity to introduce draughtproofing measures.

DOORS

Doors have a variety of apertures that allow draughts to enter. These are rarely addressed, but can make a tremendous difference to energy-efficiency. If you put your finger over a traditional keyhole on a cold day, you will notice a rush of cool air coming through. A simple, well-fitted keyhole cover (an escutcheon cover plate) can save a considerable amount of warm air leakage.

Letter plates and cat-flaps are even worse when it comes to air leakage. There are a variety of energy-efficient versions on the market which close with a rubber seal. Most of them are incongruous plastic designs but more attractive styles are available.

The simplest solution to draughtproof a letter slot is a wooden hinged flap, fitted with a spring. Even a piece of heavy fabric, insulated and weighted, can improve the situation.

Old-fashioned draught excluders (fabric 'sausages') work well at the bottom of a draughty door, and can be filled with fine gravel, bean bag balls, lentils or anything that gives a little weight and keeps it in place.

Old external doors rarely fit tightly in their frames. Over the decades they might have dropped slightly, their hinges might have loosened or the walls around them subsided. They may also swell and shrink in damp and warm weather, making them stick in the winter. Consequently, external doors will often have been periodically planed to fit so the gaps around the outside become bigger.

The simple and reversible draughtproofing solution is a rubber compression seal in a metal trim which is pinned to the door lining. This is available in most DIY stores and usually comes in brass or chrome finishes. It can be painted to match the frame but it is visually rather intrusive and not particularly effective if the gaps are large. A brush seal can also be fitted to the base of the door on the internal face, where the draughts tend to be most noticeable. They allow the door to swing open and shut, but are rather ugly.

Professional draughtproofing is a much better solution and can be fitted to old doors in a similar way to windows, either to the edge of the door or, preferably, to the frame. The position of the seal is dependant on the type used so check with the manufacturer. Always use an experienced joiner to carry out the work and opt for a good-quality seal.

Depending on the design, it may be possible to insulate an old door. Aerogel, or a similar thin insulation product, can sometimes be fitted to the internal face and covered over with plywood. Insulation boards can be fitted within the sunken panels to the inner face. This will only work for flat panels, ideally without mouldings, but can provide a simple and reversible option. If insulating an old door, try to make the work reversible.

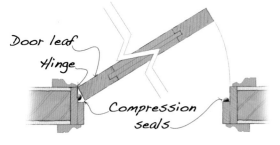

Left: Compression seals are typically fitted to the stop on the meeting side of the door frame, and the lining on the hinge side. This way they will both be compressed when the door is closed, minimising air leakage.

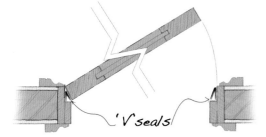

Left: 'V' seals are fitted to the door lining on all three sides.

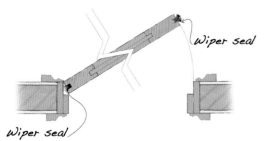

Left: Wiper seals can be fitted to the frame, but are more usually rebated into the edge of the door leaf.

Left: Old doors rarely fit tightly in their frames.

Right: Certain doors can be upgraded by fitting extra insulation and thin ply into sunken panels. This door is being monitored.

Below: A rubber compression seal pinned to the door lining, painted to match.

Below right: A brass escutcheon plate and cover.

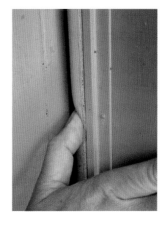

A porch should complement the existing facade and, where skilfully executed, may even enhance it. Ideally, where there is room, it is useful to provide hanging space so that wet clothes can be removed and hung within the porch, minimising the moisture that is brought into the body of the house. A small radiator to provide a background heat source, perhaps in a porch seat, can help prevent mould or mildew on clothes hanging above.

The creation of a vestibule through the addition of a door and partition is particularly suited to Victorian layouts where the front door leads to a long corridor. A glazed inner door will allow borrowed light into the interior. Ideally it should be designed to open flat against a wall to allow it to be hooked back in the warmer months when an airlock is not required.

Door curtains

Portière rods are a traditional method of hanging a curtain against a door, so that it opens and closes with it. A prop is fixed to the door leaf, which supports the end of a curtain pole, while allowing it to slide along when the door is in motion. Door curtains should be heavily insulated (➡ Heavily insulated curtains, page 80) but should not touch the floor as they will become snarled in the gap under the door.

PORCHES AND VESTIBULES

Every time an external door is opened and closed, a large volume of warm air is lost and replaced with cold air from the outside. One way of resolving this problem is to add a second door to create an 'airlock' where only one door is open at any time.

Where there is space internally, this can be achieved by creating a vestibule. Alternatively, a porch might be added to the external elevation. Whichever solution is chosen, it should be large enough so the inner and outer doors do not have to be opened simultaneously, otherwise the benefits of the airlock will be lost. By adding a porch or vestibule, the historic door can be left in its original condition, and all efforts with regard to insulation and draughtproofing can be concentrated on the new, second door. This solution is particularly useful in cutting down traffic noise on busy roads.

Above: A portière rod and door curtain.

Right: Fanlights, like this simple example in a Georgian terraced house in a London conservation area, were first introduced in the 1720s to bring natural light into hallways.

Right: A porch added to
a Victorian house adds
character and helps keep
out the cold.

Below: A new porch is fitted
to a timber-framed house in
Oxfordshire.

Opposite: A lime-rendered timber-framed house.

Below right: Regional variations in walling and other materials make every streetscape unique.

6
Walls

Traditional solid walls pose huge questions when it comes to deciding on insulation, many of which remain unresolved. In some situations, wall insulation may be best avoided. Inappropriate solutions risk considerable damage to the building's structure, character and the wellbeing of its occupants.

Old walls not only vary enormously in their thickness and construction, but their performance differs according to their orientation and location. What they have in common is that, until about a hundred years ago, they were constructed using permeable materials including lime mortars, renders and plasters so they are able to breathe. Breathability allows water, in the form of vapour or liquid, to pass readily through the body of the wall and escape, or be redistributed within it.

With thermal insulation at the top of the eco agenda, many firms are offering quick and easy solutions for insulating old walls without understanding the long-term consequences. When it comes to insulating solid walls, it is crucial to find a solution that is compatible with their breathable characteristics, rather than imposing a system that is designed for modern cavity construction.

While adding insulation can improve the thermal efficiency of walls in the short term, it potentially acts as a barrier to the natural breathing process, trapping moisture and causing serious condensation within the thickness of the wall. Wind-driven rain poses a particular risk with certain systems, as solid walls are less able to dry out once insulation has been installed. Not only are

Below: Breathing walls are given special dispensation under the Building Regulations.

damp walls less thermally efficient, but often the problems are hidden from view and remain undetected, resulting in decay and mould growth which is damaging to the building's fabric and to human health.

BUILDING REGULATIONS

In 1965, when U-values were first introduced, new walls had to meet a target of 1.7W/m²K. This figure has gradually been tightened. Under the circumstances listed in Chapter 2, page 29, existing walls must be upgraded to comply with current U-values, although the regulations accept that internal insulation is not appropriate if it reduces the floor area by more than 5 per cent.

The Building Regulations recognise that 'buildings of traditional construction with permeable fabric' need to be treated in a way that allows them to breathe. The regulations therefore should not require the use of a non-breathable type of insulation with an old building. They go on to say that any alterations should 'improve energy-efficiency as far as is reasonably practicable'. By quoting this wording to the building control officer, there should be room for negotiation when seeking a compatible solution.

Above: Leaking rainwater goods cause water to run down walls, resulting in damage and decay to the building's structure; wet walls are also thermally inefficient.

WET WALLS ARE COLD

A damp wall will be dramatically less thermally efficient than a dry wall, as water is a better thermal conductor and will allow heat to pass through. SPAB research suggests that up to 40 per cent more heat is lost through a damp wall compared to a dry wall. Before even considering any type of wall insulation, it is essential to ensure your existing walls are dry by checking their condition, addressing any maintenance issues and allowing them to 'breathe' through the use of lime or earth mortars, renders and plasters.

If the house has exposed masonry with pointing:
> Check the pointing is in good order.
> Where the pointing has been replaced with cement and is trapping damp, consider replacing with lime so the wall can breathe.

If the house is rendered:
> Check whether the surface of the render is cracked – even small cracks will draw in rain via capillary action.
> If the render is cement, investigate whether it is trapping moisture and, if so, replace with a lime render.
> If it is lime render, check whether it is finished with a breathable paint such as limewash. Modern masonry paints can stop a lime render from breathing.

Above: Cement pointing is carefully removed from this early nineteenth-century wall to allow it to breathe and dry out. Once repaired, it will be repointed with traditional lime mortar.

It is worth monitoring the performance of gutters, downpipes and gullies during heavy rain to ensure they are channelling water away rather than allowing it to run down the wall. Consider whether leaking drains or pipes, raised external ground levels or other factors are contributing to dampness in the wall.

If you are in any doubt whether walls are damp, get them checked by a competent surveyor specialising in solid-wall construction. Do not rely on a twin probe or non-invasive electrical moisture meter on the inside face of the wall: either could be picking up surface condensation, salts or even foil-backed plasterboard.

Once the causes of damp problems have been resolved, the thermal performance of the wall may be strikingly improved without the need to add insulation.

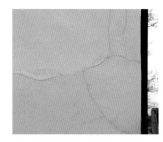

Location, location, location

In certain exposed locations, where buildings are regularly subjected to wind-driven rain, it may be more effective to focus on simply weatherproofing the outside to keep the wall dry, rather than trying to insulate the inside. In order to keep water out, various traditions have evolved along the west coast of the UK such as slate-hanging and roughcasting. The use of a lime roughcast covers any cracks in the wall and blocks the majority of wind-driven rain. The knobbly texture vastly increases the surface area, and any water that is absorbed is rapidly evaporated through its vapour-permeable structure after a downpour of rain. Over the last hundred years, the fashion for removing these 'rainscreens' and protective coatings, often to expose the rubble stone, has completely ignored their value in terms of keeping the wall dry. More recently, rubble walls have been repointed or rendered with hard cement-based materials, which tend to trap moisture behind them. By removing external cementitious finishes and replacing

with traditional, vapour-permeable techniques, the thermal efficiency of a wall in an exposed location may be dramatically improved (➡ Which houses are at risk?, page 108).

Above right: A lime roughcast is a good way of minimising the effects of wind-driven rain and maximising evaporation to a damp wall.

Left: Slate-hanging in a Cornish coastal town.

How does a wet wall dry out?

Assuming all defects have been resolved, such as leaking rainwater goods or defective pointing, walls generally dry out through the following mechanisms:

> External evaporation: the most effective drying mechanism is through evaporation from the external surface, aided by the action of wind and sun.
> Vapour diffusion, driven by a vapour pressure differential that pushes moisture vapour from within the wall towards the internal or external surface, dependent on where the pressure is lowest.
> Heat flow via heat loss from the internal environment converts liquid water in the core into water vapour, which can then be diffused.
> Internal evaporation: particularly damp walls may also evaporate moisture through the internal surface, provided it is plastered and decorated with breathable materials.

All of these mechanisms rely on the wall being able to breathe, hence permeable finishes play an important role in keeping the wall dry.

Top left: Even hairline cracks in cement renders can cause walls to become damp.

Above left: Defective rainwater goods are a primary cause of penetrating damp.

Above: This exposed building in Orkney absorbs and evaporates moisture through its breathable lime finish.

How wet does your wall get?

It is estimated that 30 per cent of driving rain splashes off vertical wall surfaces. The remaining 70 per cent could potentially be absorbed into the wall, depending on a variety of factors, but most importantly:

> Location: buildings on the UK's west coast receive much higher levels of rainfall.
> Orientation: south-westerly elevations are generally exposed to greater levels of driving rain due to wind direction.
> Wall surface: the moisture-absorption characteristics of a particular wall surface dictate how much moisture is absorbed. Granite has a very low rate of absorption, compared to a soft stone or brick. A lime render or breathable cladding should be considered on exposed walls with high wicking characteristics.
> Via defective mortar joints and cracks.

Below: These exposed clifftop houses in Cornwall receive high levels of driving rain.

HOW DO WALLS COMPARE?

It has long been assumed that old walls are cold walls, compared to modern construction with insulated cavities. But how much do we really know? For instance, cob walls (made of earth and straw) anecdotally perform extremely well, keeping occupants warm in winter and cool in summer. Yet, in theory, they do not meet current Building Regulations for U-values.

The SPAB, along with other heritage bodies, has been monitoring the U-values of traditional walls for several years. The results have been compared with existing data for traditionally constructed walls and, in the majority of cases, the traditional wall has performed much better than expected. So what type of construction performs best?

> Thicker walls perform better than thin walls. For instance, rubble stone and cob, built to thicknesses typically of 600mm upwards, perform better than 9-inch (225mm) brickwork.
> Walls with sound external lime renders or traditional rainscreens such as tile-hanging or weatherboarding. These help to keep the core of the wall dry, particularly in exposed situations.

The lime test

To check whether mortar or render is composed of lime (as opposed to cement), place the pointed tip of a sharp knife against the wall and lean on it. If the tip sinks in, it is most likely lime; if it does not, it is almost certainly cement. Cement mortars and renders may contribute to dampness within a wall, particularly if they are in poor condition. In such cases, replacement with a lime-based mortar or render will allow the wall to dry out over time and will improve the thermal efficiency of the structure

The tip of a blade sinks into lime mortar (left), but cannot penetrate cement (right).

Take care that the blade does not suddenly snap shut.

> Walls containing a large proportion of lime or earth mortar. Mortar is less thermally conductive than stone, so rubble-stone walls with a larger proportion of mortar, especially at their core, are likely to out-perform ashlar or brick walls which have narrow mortar joints.
> Walls made of less conductive material. For instance, limestone generally performs better than sandstone due to density. Daub and cob, both mixed with straw, are better insulators than brick and stone.
> Walls with minimal gaps. Traditional timber-framed houses often have gaps around the edges of the infill panels and in the joints of the frame, making them less airtight and more draughty. Heat is transferred many times faster by convection though a crack than by conduction though solid materials.
> Walls lined internally with an unventilated airspace – for instance, timber lining on studs, lath and plaster, or dry-lined plasterboard.
> Walls with smaller windows and fewer openings.
> Dry walls always perform better than damp walls: regular maintenance is crucial.

Recorded U-values

Results from the SPAB's in-situ monitoring of existing solid walls have shown that certain construction types perform much better in reality than their expected, theoretically calculated U-values. 'Heat flux monitors' and temperature sensors were fixed to a variety of wall types to measure the heat flow, or heat loss, through the wall over a two-week period during the winter months. The table (below right) shows some average results.

Rubble-stone walls (which are constructed with random-sized stones) contain large air voids, lumps of earth and lime-based mortars which improve the insulation qualities of the wall. Calculated U-values do not necessarily take account of this. Wattle and daub is also a better insulator than is theoretically assumed. Standard U-value calculation programmes were designed to simulate modern materials such as bricks which are largely predictable.

With results gained from around the country, the SPAB is building a database of U-values for a wide variety of traditional materials and construction types. This will help to improve the accuracy of computer modelling in the future and inform decisions made when retrofitting for insulation.

Above: Thick rubble-stone walls as in this house in Lancashire, with a large volume of lime mortar, perform better than ashlar walls.

Above: Heat flux monitors used to measure in-situ U-values.

Above: 9-inch brick walls with large sashes have a poorer thermal performance than thick rubble-stone walls with small window openings.

Wall type	Approx. width (inc. plaster)	Theoretical U-value	In-situ U-value (average)
Rubble limestone	600mm	1.79	1.19
Rubble sandstone	600mm	2.31	1.63
Wattle and daub	140mm	2.19	1.69
Brick, 13½ inch	380mm	1.52	1.48
Brick, 9 inch	248mm	2.10	2.13

INSULATING SOLID WALLS

Wall insulation in solid-walled structures is a highly controversial and technically difficult issue. There is much disagreement about how it should be done, and some experts suggest that many of the products on the market will create problems of dampness and mould growth in the future.

If you have old lime plaster internally or render externally you should not be removing it or covering it with materials that might damage it. Much of the beauty of an old room can come from gently uneven plasterwork. Replacing it or covering it with a flat and lifeless modern insulation material can destroy a character that may have taken hundreds of years to develop. Equally, some old buildings will have historic external render or, in some parts of the country, pargetting. This should not be put at risk simply by a desire to improve energy-efficiency.

Concerns regarding structural failure resulting from insulation mean a growing number of building professionals are hesitant as to whether it should be attempted at all. It is almost impossible to predict the effect of insulation on a solid wall over a long period of time. The factors that determine the outcome are so numerous and unique to each individual building they are impossible to simulate fully or understand.

The first question to consider is whether wall insulation is appropriate or practical. Analyse the benefits and ask: 'What difference will wall insulation really make?' If the wall area is relatively small compared to the glazed areas and doorways, and insulation is technically difficult to achieve, it may be best to leave the wall well alone; for example, in a mid-terrace house with large sash windows. Conversely, an end of terrace will usually have a large external gable wall that may be losing an unacceptable amount of heat.

Where wall insulation is considered necessary, a huge number of products and systems are now available. While these can perform exceptionally well when used in conjunction with modern walls, many are inappropriate for older buildings. Genuinely breathable products are far more compatible with solid walls as they do not trap damp, although they do rely on good detailing and are not appropriate for all situations. Do not opt for the cheapest 'quick fix' solution as it may be a false economy in the longer term if it causes damage to the structure or devalues the house due to loss of historic

Opposite: If the window area forms a large proportion of the elevation, wall insulation is of little benefit.

Above: Large gable ends with few window or door openings may be worth insulating in certain cases.

If in doubt, leave it out

An old house may have been around for centuries and, with careful maintenance and informed choices, last for many more. Never take a gamble on so-called 'improvements' that may compromise its longevity, particularly with regard to insulation. If in any doubt, defer the decision for a few years until products and systems have been tried and tested, and there is a better general understanding of the associated problems.

Above: Every old house has a unique set of challenges. This mid-terrace stone building in Swanage, Dorset, has a large proportion of glazing to the front elevation, and the technical challenges of wall insulation are unlikely to be worth the risk.

features. If you are planning to insulate your walls, take impartial advice from a qualified person specialising in traditional construction.

Inside or out?

There are generally just two options for improving the thermal performance of solid walls in old houses: insulating externally or internally. Both usually result in the loss of period features. The decision about where to insulate must also take into account a host of technical issues, including wall type, location and exposure, while each building type needs to be considered separately. In some cases a combination of external and internal insulation, used on different elevations, may be an option.

Whichever solution is finally agreed, it is crucial that it is well detailed and supervised by professionals with expertise in the type of building involved. The more complex the solution, the more care needs to be taken when installing or fitting, so choice of contractor, coupled with on-site supervision, becomes critical. Above all, always check that the solution proposed is ultimately compatible with the building's fabric.

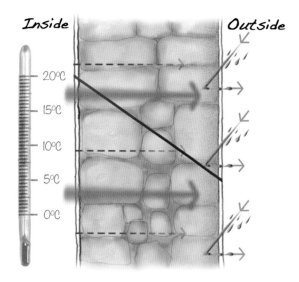

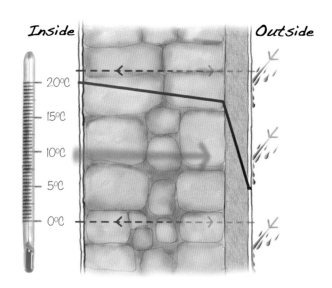

Above: Solid uninsulated walls lose heat via conductivity. This section through a rubble-stone wall shows the internal temperature is 20°C and the external air temperature is 5°C – a typical winter scenario. A graph showing the temperature gradient is plotted over the top, indicated by the red/blue line. In exposed situations, driving rain may penetrate the outside surface and be drawn in via capillary action. Over time the absorbed water evaporates, due to vapour pressure differential, assisted by heat flow through the wall.

Above: When external insulation is added, the temperature gradient is dramatically altered. The red/blue line shows how the wall remains warm, dropping just a few degrees in temperature across its width, with the majority of the temperature drop occurring across the insulation. A properly specified external insulation should be breathable to allow the passage of water vapour from inside to outside, but resist the absorption of driving rain the other way.

Right: External wall insulation can sometimes be difficult, with complex features such as bay windows, stone cills or narrow window frames. The risk of incomplete insulation coverage can lead to thermal bridging, resulting in internal condensation and mould.

EXTERNAL INSULATION

Where wall insulation is considered necessary and appropriate, external insulation is technically a better option than internal insulation in most situations. It is like wrapping your body in a thick duvet to keep all the heat inside. By keeping the mass of the wall warm, the risk of interstitial condensation (see page 106) is virtually eliminated. This is good news where the building has a rendered or clad facade, as it can potentially be insulated and re-rendered without too much change to the appearance of the building. It is not the case if the house is constructed of decorative brickwork, has fine detailing or an exposed timber frame with infill panels. External insulation can be particularly unsatisfactory if the building is part of an unspoilt terrace where the architectural cohesion of the rest of the row would be destroyed by changing the outside of a single dwelling.

External insulation: key issues

> Any insulation system to a solid-walled structure should consider breathability, to allow the movement of moisture through the wall, particularly at the base.

> Always resolve any existing damp problems before insulating, otherwise residual and continuing dampness will be trapped inside the wall.

> By insulating on the outside, the thickness of the wall will increase. This will almost certainly mean an adjustment to roof details such as at the eaves and verge to provide a wider overhang.

> If the rafters need to be extended to accommodate the extra thickness of the wall, check they will not obstruct outward-opening windows or doors.

> The added thickness of external insulation may result in the walls oversailing property boundaries, or alleyways and footpaths between buildings becoming too narrow. This can pose legal, planning and access issues.

> Details around window and door openings need careful consideration to ensure a neat finish and continuity without any gaps or thermal bridging.

> Any insulation to window and door reveals should allow their frames to be removed for repair or renewal in the future.

> The position of window frames may need to be altered to avoid the window being set back too far within the facade.

> Gutters, downpipes, soil pipes and cables running down the face of the wall must be removed and reinstalled.

> Rainwater gullies at the base of the wall may need to be re-sited.

> Boiler flues, overflow pipes and condensate pipes may need extending.

> Where decorative front elevations preclude external insulation, consider external insulation to the other elevations such as end gables and the rear of the building.

> Consideration should be given to how the bottom of the insulation will terminate. If it is taken down to the ground there may be a risk of moisture tracking up through capillary action. If the insulation is stopped before the base of the wall there will be an ugly step and a danger of thermal bridging.

> Carefully consider any detailing to parapets and chimneys.

Above: External insulation must be carefully thought through as it will impact on various details. Here, the rear of a typical terrace is shown before and after insulation. The insulation has been brought down to incorporate the majority of the wall, but stops short as an extension is to be added to the house in the future. Note that traditional wooden sash windows have been reinstated.

INTERNAL INSULATION

Where external insulation is not appropriate, internal insulation may be an alternative. While the job appears to be simple, it presents a host of technical and aesthetic difficulties.

Adding insulation to internal wall surfaces may involve the loss of original period features such as cornicing, skirtings and architraves. For a house with uneven walls and soft undulating lime plaster, most insulation systems will further destroy the character of the interior by leaving it with flat and lifeless finishes. Beside the aesthetic consequences for the historic fabric, the technical ramifications of an inappropriate system may be far more damaging due to increased damp levels.

With an ill-conceived or poorly installed system, there are two major risks: interstitial condensation caused by water vapour from within the room, and increased dampness due to driving rain. Both can result in serious structural issues as there is a very real possibility that any timber elements within the wall, such as embedded joist ends, bonding timbers and lintels, will rot due to the increased moisture content.

Interstitial condensation

Insulation on the inner face changes the performance of the wall by preventing heat from inside the building warming up the mass of the masonry. If, as a result, the temperature of the stone or brick drops to dewpoint, any water vapour passing through the interior surfaces of the insulation system, as well as the vapour already in the wall, will condense. This is referred to as interstitial condensation (⟹ Interstitial condensation, page 47), as opposed to surface condensation. It can be disastrous, as moisture builds up in areas that are impossible to see and difficult to access.

Vapour control layer (VCL)

Most modern internal insulation systems incorporate a vapour control layer (VCL), designed to minimise moisture vapour passing through from the room to the wall. For instance, insulated studwork with mineral wool quilts or batts relies on a separate membrane applied to the warm side. The foil face of a foam board acts as a VCL provided it is properly taped at all junctions. In both cases, plasterboard is usually applied over the top. In theory VCLs should work but, in reality, they rarely provide a vapour-tight layer.

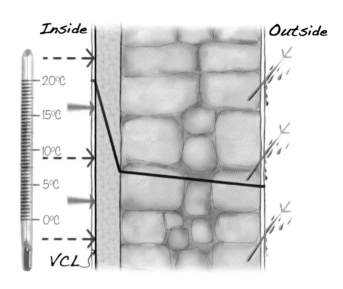

Above: Non-breathable internal wall insulation such as foam board relies on an effective VCL. This is usually incorporated in the board itself, and airtight tape should be applied around any junctions. This, in theory, will stop water vapour from entering the wall, but is a potentially risky strategy when used in conjunction with a solid wall. The red/blue line indicates the temperature drop across the insulation, leaving the masonry cold and vulnerable to interstitial condensation.

VCLs are often poorly installed and not properly sealed at the junctions and edges. Given that they are such a crucial part of the system, they are extremely vulnerable to damage, such as the installation of new wall sockets or nails driven through to hang a picture. Any breach of a VCL could result in interstitial condensation which becomes trapped and unable to dry out (⟹ Vapour control layer, page 48).

Driving rain

As well as interstitial condensation, there is an even more complex problem with VCLs that is often overlooked. When wind-driven rain hits the external face of a wall, it may be drawn in via capillary action, dependent on the wicking characteristics of the brick or stone. In certain circumstances, rain may track across a solid wall and a breathable inner face becomes crucial to allow moisture to evaporate into the room. If a VCL or impermeable system has been inserted, moisture in the core may become trapped behind it and unable to escape.

Top: Adding internal insulation to areas such as stairwells can make them too narrow.

Above: Systems such as this mineral wool insulation rely on vapour control layers fitted over the top to prevent interstitial condensation.

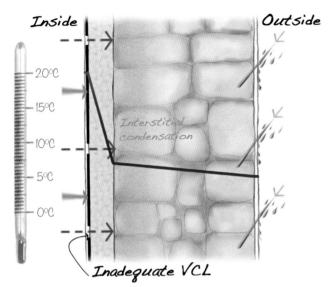

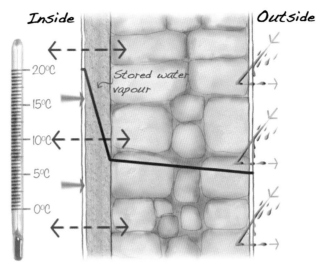

Above: When the VCL is punctured, poorly detailed or not properly taped, water vapour can pass through it and is likely to condense on, or within, the cold masonry wall when it reaches dewpoint temperature. This will cause interstitial condensation where it cannot be seen, and cannot escape.

Above: Wood fibreboard is an option for internal insulation on solid walls. Unlike foam boards, its hygroscopic properties allow it to store a certain amount of water vapour, stopping it from reaching the cold masonry and condensing. It also allows a degree of moisture movement and evaporation in both directions. When the internal humidity drops, the stored vapour can evaporate harmlessly back into the room. Too much water vapour would eventually cause saturation of the insulation, and the formation of interstitial condensation.

Right: If wind-driven rain tracks through the wall it can become trapped behind impermeable insulation such as foam board.

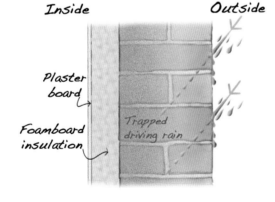

Above: Driving rain can cause problems with internally insulated houses, especially systems incorporating a vapour control layer.

Right: Breathable insulation with good hygroscopic properties such as wood fibreboard will wick wind-driven moisture away from the masonry and allow it to evaporate into the room.

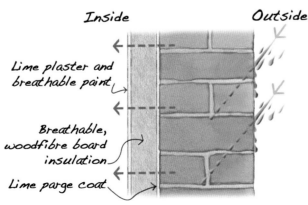

> masonry walls with high wicking characteristics lacking breathable renders or rainscreens
> thin walls such as those in historic timber-framed buildings

In such instances, where the core of the wall may already be damp, internal insulation can exacerbate the problem, particularly non-breathable systems or those incorporating a VCL. If internal insulation is added, it separates the masonry wall from the internal heated environment and, without heat flow across the masonry, the mechanisms for drying out the core become more limited.

Less is more

If the wall is generally dry and well maintained, but exposed to high levels of driving rain, it may be possible to add a limited amount of breathable internal insulation. By using a product that gives a total wall U-value of no less than 0.4 W/m^2K, some heat from the internal environment will be able to pass through the insulation and raise the wall temperature just enough to prevent moisture build-up. Its breathable characteristics will also allow dampness to evaporate back into the room in the event of moisture tracking across the core. These U-values do not meet Building Regulations, but the thermal efficiency will still be improved while potential risks will be avoided.

Manufacturers of internal insulation systems may recommend treating the outside face of the wall with a breathable hydrophobic primer to limit wind-driven rain entering the core, particularly in exposed locations. These treatments are non-reversible and, as such, should be treated with caution. Some formulations can reduce, if not stop, breathability, trapping moisture and causing

Better to be breathable

Carefully detailed breathable systems with good density and hygroscopicity offer a safer and more robust option than impermeable internal insulation on most solid walls. Where materials such as foam board may trap moisture at the interface between the insulation and the cold wall, a material such as wood fibreboard, fitted against the wall, will store any excess water vapour from the internal environment. In situations where driving rain has tracked across the wall, dampness can be wicked away and evaporated back into the room. No VCL is required, although certain wood fibreboards designed for this purpose contain a silicate layer which is a vapour-retarder, discouraging moisture from the room entering the wall, while still allowing it to breathe.

Which houses are at risk?

Installing internal insulation comes with problems, some of which can be reduced or even overcome through careful specification and good workmanship. But certain buildings are at much greater risk than others, and internal insulation should be minimised or avoided in the following situations:

> buildings with inherent or unresolved damp problems
> houses in exposed locations with high levels of wind-driven rain

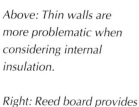

Above: Thin walls are more problematic when considering internal insulation.

Right: Reed board provides some insulation, and is an ideal substrate for lime plaster. It is not sufficient to cause interstitial condensation in most applications.

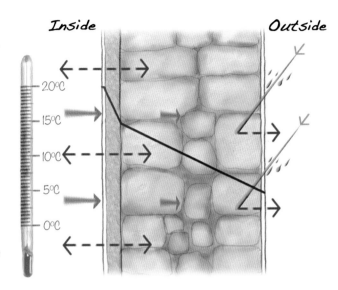

Right: In exposed situations risks may be minimised by using less internal insulation. Greater heat loss will raise the temperature in the core of the wall, pushing the dewpoint temperature towards the external face and interstitial condensation may be averted. The heat flow will also assist in evaporating wind-driven rain absorbed in the wall. Provided the internal insulation is fully breathable, and does not incorporate a VCL, vapour can evaporate in both directions.

the breakdown of softer materials. It may be better to consider a rainscreen type of cladding or a breathable render as an alternative.

Preparing the wall

With internal space at a premium, wall plaster is often removed to gain a few extra millimetres before internal insulation is added. Think carefully before removing original lime plaster as it leads to the loss of historic fabric, involves further work and creates more dust and disruption. In addition, the old plaster must be disposed of, which results in extra cost and waste going to landfill. If removing gypsum plaster there are strict rules regarding its disposal due to the release of hydrogen sulphide gas.

Where plaster is removed, it is generally recommended that a thin 'parge' coat of lime plaster is applied to the wall to fill cracks and holes and thus prevent any thermal bridging or air leakage as well as giving a level base from which to work. This also provides a moisture-

Party walls

When adding internal insulation to a house that is attached to another, party walls have to be carefully considered. This plan of a terrace row illustrates three different situations: Junction A shows an insulated internal face that does not return along the party wall, creating a thermal bridge where heat can escape. Junction B shows the insulation returned all the way to the chimney breast, making it less visually obtrusive. Junction C shows insulation returned 600mm along the party wall, creating an awkward step in the wall. Both B and C will reduce heat loss at the junction. A similar problem occurs when converting loft spaces, as the neighbouring space is often unheated. In such cases, it will be necessary to treat the party wall as an external wall and insulate it in its entirety.

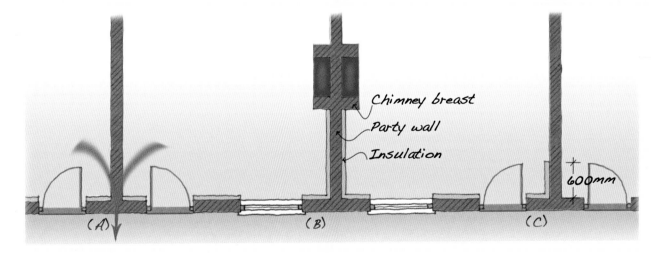

buffer to the wall surface, absorbing any vapour or condensation. Whether plaster is removed or not, any significant holes should always be filled or 'dubbed out' with a lime mortar to minimise air voids. It is vital that any new lime plaster is allowed to carbonate fully and dry before insulation is fitted over the top. A thin 10mm parge coat may dry within days, but thicker areas may require weeks to dry, depending on environmental conditions.

Before insulating internally, it is good practice to take off gypsum plaster as it breaks down when it gets damp. Old wallpaper should be stripped as it provides nutrients for mould growth and impermeable paints should also be removed.

Embedded joist ends

One of the greatest risks of internal insulation is future decay to embedded joist and beam ends due to an increase in the moisture content of the surrounding masonry. Many internal retrofits will stop the insulation at the floor or ceiling junction. This creates a thermal bridge at the masonry between the joists within the floor void, encouraging condensation at a particularly vulnerable point in the wall.

More rigorous retrofits usually involve lifting the floorboards at the edge of the room and continuing the insulation down between the joists. Some internal insulation systems recommend taping the junction between the insulation and the sides of joists. Airtightness around

Right: Traditionally, timber joist ends were set into the masonry of the external wall.

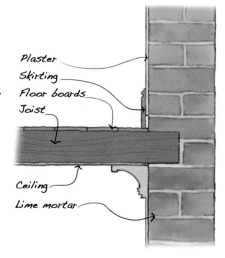

Right: Internal insulation often stops at the floor and the ceiling, leaving a thermal bridge in the masonry between the joists. This will attract condensation and may rot timber joist ends.

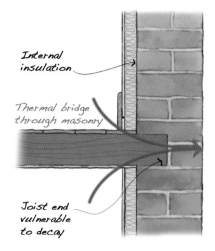

Top: Before internal insulation is applied, gypsum plaster should ideally be removed.

Above: Before internal insulation is fitted, a lime 'parge' coat should be applied to the masonry to buffer any moisture at the interface.

Right: Most internal insulation systems recommend lifting boards and cutting back the ceiling to continue the insulation around the joists. This is extremely invasive if the house has historic finishes. While the thermal bridge is minimised, the joists still provide a potential path for moisture, possibly leaving them vulnerable to decay in the future.

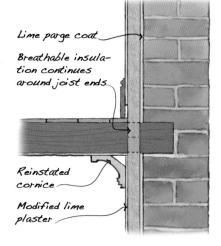

this junction is important to minimise water vapour passing through. It must not be forgotten, however, that the timber joist or beam is hygroscopic and will allow a certain amount of moisture to travel along it, meeting the cold masonry where the structural timber ends in the core of the wall.

The longevity of joist and beam ends is dependent on minimising both condensation and driving rain, and keeping the wall as dry as possible. Different insulation systems will recommend different treatments, but the long-term effect on embedded timbers is difficult to predict as there are so many complex factors involved. Monitoring is possible with moisture probes and may, in certain circumstances, be worth the additional cost. In a worst-case scenario, joist-end decay could go on unde-tected behind internal insulation for many years until structural failure becomes apparent.

Window and door reveals

When walls are insulated on the inside, the treatment of window reveals is problematic. If left uninsulated, they can act as a thermal bridge, yet the thickness of the window frame usually limits the insulation that can be fixed to the reveal. The diagrams below show uninsulated reveals to the left, where heat loss is at its greatest. The reveals to the right have a thin layer of insulation, reducing the thermal bridge. Remember to allow for the thickness of the plaster on top of any insulation. The head of the window will also act as a thermal bridge and needs to be considered. Where insulation covers over a wooden lintel, it may become vulnerable to changes in moisture content. Rubble-stone walls usually have splayed reveals, but brick walls usually have square reveals which can become 'tunnel-like' if internal insulation is added.

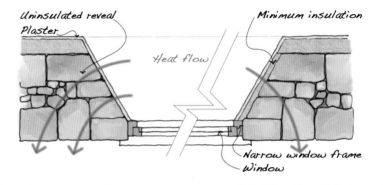

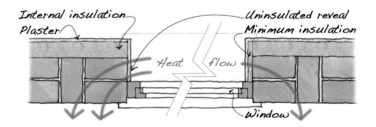

Internal insulation: issues

> Before opting for any internal insulation system, ask the company or professional involved about the risks of interstitial condensation. Ask for a hygrothermal analysis of the solution they are proposing, and check this is not based on a Glaser diagram (➡ Analysis, page 47).

> Consider the amount of internal insulation that is safe to use, depending on the location and wicking characteristics of the wall. Houses in exposed locations should be insulated to a lesser degree, if at all.

> Breathable insulation products with good hygroscopic properties are generally the most suitable for solid walls.

> Evaluate whether a VCL is appropriate for a particular situation and, if it is, take care not to puncture or damage it.

> Detailing around joist ends is complex. There are a variety of details dependent on the insulation system used but these require careful consideration.

> Internal floor area will be reduced. This is a particular consideration in smaller houses and where maintaining passageway or staircase widths is crucial.

> Features such as skirtings, cornices and architraves will need to be removed.

> Original plaster and paint finishes will be hidden, and inevitably damaged or destroyed.

> Electrical sockets and switches, pipes and radiators fixed to external walls will need to be repositioned. Where electrical outlets remain on insulated walls they should be surface-mounted to avoid compromising the performance of the insulation. In many cases, extensive rewiring and plumbing alterations will be required.

> Detailing around window and door openings must be meticulous to avoid thermal bridging and air leakage.

> Detailing around existing fireplaces needs to be carefully thought through.

> The effect of 'thermal mass' in masonry walls is lost after internal insulation has been fitted.

> Hanging cupboards off internally insulated walls can be problematic with some systems.

Left: Internal insulation can significantly reduce floor area.

INSULATING SYSTEMS

Numerous materials and systems are available for insulating masonry walls (➡ Thermal insulation, page 49). There is no one solution for all buildings and what is used will depend on the breathability required, the space available, the cost and the thermal performance sought. All systems should be installed to manufacturer's instructions.

Calcium silicate board – internal

Before fitting, internal plaster is removed and a 20mm lime-based levelling coat is spread. Once fully cured, a permeable adhesive is applied and the board is pressed on to it, eliminating any air pockets where vapour could otherwise collect and condense. Once the adhesive has set, the boards are coated with a lime-based plaster and breathable paint.

Left: Calcium silicate board is applied to wall adhesive.

Reed board – internal

This can be fixed relatively easily directly to the inner face of the external wall using plastic washers and stainless steel screws or, better still, non-metallic fixing. As each reed contains a large proportion of trapped air, the board performs surprisingly well. In recent SPAB monitoring tests, reed board achieved good results in terms of reducing heat loss, yet a hygrothermal analysis suggests it is unlikely to cause interstitial condensation. Unlike most other products, it is very flexible and therefore able to follow the undulations of a wall that is not straight. It has the added advantage of providing an ideal substrate for lime plaster, even an insulating lime plaster.

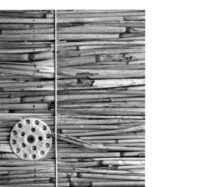

Left: Reed board with fixing.

Below: Damp-spray cellulose insulation application (left) and levelling (right).

Cellulose insulation – internal

There are two options when using cellulose to insulate walls: loose fill or damp spray. Both methods rely on timber stud work being fixed to the wall. When loose-fill cellulose is used, plasterboard is fixed to the studs and holes are drilled into it through which the dry cellulose is blown into the gap between the wall and the board. Some settlement of the material may occur. With wet spray, water and sometimes an adhesive is added to the cellulose and it is sprayed directly on to the wall before being levelled off to the depth of the studs. It must then be allowed to dry before being covered with plasterboard. This method helps seal voids and eliminates settling.

Right: Wood fibreboard incorporating a wood wool batt is fitted internally to a solid brick wall.

Centre: Layers of wood fibreboard fixed externally to a solid brick wall with battens are used to create a cavity behind timber rainscreen cladding.

Bottom: Insulated studwork systems are a standard internal solution; however, the materials used are rarely breathable so should be carefully detailed and used with caution on a solid wall.

Wood fibreboards – internal

Some are specifically designed for internal use on masonry walls and incorporate a silicate layer to retard moisture vapour. Other products are integrated with a layer of wood wool, allowing the board to be pressed against the uneven masonry substrate to fill voids. When used internally, wood fibreboards should be sealed at any cut junctions using airtightness tape. The whole surface is then coated with mesh-reinforced modified lime plasters.

Wood fibreboards – external

A variety of natural wood fibreboard insulation systems is now available for the external insulation of solid walls. They can be used to create a breathable, continuous and unbridged thermal shell. Each tends to be designed for specific purposes and, depending on the type of board used, they can be clad with timber and other materials or finished with breathable render.

The boards are fixed with either insulated screw fixings or special bonding mortar. Some are specially designed to resist driving rain and are tongue-and-grooved to ensure unbroken insulation. Always ensure the tongue is pointing upwards to prevent water from collecting in the groove.

Insulated studwork – internal

There are various ways of insulating using studwork. The most basic is to fix timber studs to the wall at intervals with insulation placed between them. Insulated plasterboard is then fixed over the face of these which reduces the effects of any thermal bridging through the timber. Proprietary systems employ engineered studs composed of extruded polystyrene bonded to oriented strand board (OSB) rather than timber studs, thus preventing thermal bridging.

More advanced stud dry-lining systems consist of lightweight metal frames on to which a variety of insulation materials and plasterboard finishes may be fixed. These have the potential to introduce a significant thermal bridge so must be faced with insulation material. Direct contact between polystyrene insulation and PVC cables should be avoided as plasticisers in PVC may migrate into the polystyrene causing it to shrink and cables to become brittle.

Insulating lime plasters – internal and external

The market for insulating render systems is growing, and there are numerous products available. Many will claim to be breathable or microporous, but to ensure compatibility with a solid-walled structure aim for a product that is lime-based, usually developed by a lime-plaster supplier with experience in the field.

Products are available in both non-hydraulic and hydraulic lime forms mixed with various types of insulating fibres or granules. Non-hydraulic lime renders are far weaker and therefore more suited to soft and weak substrates as they offer greater breathability. They are delivered as a wet mix, and can be ordered by the bag or by the tonne. They usually require 'knocking up' on site before use to create better workability. Non-hydraulic mixes take longer to set as they rely wholly on the absorption of CO_2 and will be more vulnerable to frost, limiting the times they can be used.

More commonly, hydraulic limes form the base of insulating renders. These come in a powder form and require mixing with water on site just before use. Always ask what strength of lime is present, and avoid anything greater than NHL3.5 (➡ Using lime, page 14).

Foamed glass is commonly used as an insulating aggregate, as it has high crushing strength and low water absorption. The foamed glass beads are lightweight and highly porous with a closed-cell structure, trapping air in the mix.

Hemp fibre is another common additive that gives lime render an insulating property. This is a highly sustainable material and has the added advantage of locking up CO_2 in its production. Its organic nature is vulnerable to mould growth if, for any reason, the insulating render is applied too thickly and fails to carbonate. Carefully follow manufacturer's instructions regarding the maximum thickness of each coat and ensure each layer has properly carbonated before the next is applied. Hemp-based renders have become particularly popular as they have minimal shrinkage compared to traditional lime renders.

Cork-lime insulating renders are also gaining popularity and are similar in many respects to hemp-lime renders. Cork is less hygroscopic than hemp and is claimed to have better fire resistance.

With insulating plasters, other additives may be present depending on the product – for instance, cellulose, starches and gums which act as natural swelling polymers to reduce shrinkage. Non-hydraulic lime renders usually contain 'pozzolanic' additives to speed up the set.

Depending on the system used, the finish coat may contain hydrophobic agents to reduce water absorption. In order to maximise breathability, and allow any moisture within the fabric to escape, it is important to finish the external render surface with a 'vapour open' texture. This is usually achieved by using a plastic or wooden plasterer's trowel, or float.

Insulating renders can usually be applied to a maximum thickness of 25mm in one application. Once fully carbonated, additional layers can be added to build up the desired thickness and improve thermal efficiency as required. It is crucial to allow each coat to dry before the next application.

The manufacturers of breathable insulating plasters and renders claim that they can provide a 30 per cent heat loss improvement over the normal lime equivalent, though research is ongoing into this claim.

Above and left: Hemp lime plaster being prepared.

Insulating lime render: key issues

When selecting an insulating lime render, ask the manufacturer the following questions:

> Is it lime-based? If so, is it hydraulic or non-hydraulic?
> What is the insulating additive?
> What is its permeability?
> How is it finished (can a traditional limewash be used)?
> Is it suitable for your particular substrate?
> Is it easy to apply?
> What is its shelf-life?
> How thickly can it be applied in a single application?
> How long before a second coat can be applied?
> Is it suitable for internal and external use?
> Is interstitial condensation a risk when it is used internally?
> How do you avoid failure?

Left: These walls have been drilled for cavity fill and the holes have been plugged.

INSULATING CAVITY WALLS

Although we associate cavity walls with modern buildings, the first cavity walls date back to the mid-nineteenth century, if not earlier. These were designed not for insulation purposes but to resist penetrating damp. In recent years the practice of retrospective cavity fill has become widespread and is generally regarded as a cheap means of improving the U-value of a cavity wall. It is carried out by drilling a series of holes, about 22mm diameter, every metre across the external wall horizontally and vertically. The installer then blows in either loose-fill polystyrene bead, mineral wool or a foam insulant.

Cavity wall: key issues

> Make sure you use a qualified and registered installer, who will carry out a survey before the work starts, to inspect the condition and suitability of the cavity and wall ties.
> If you have a suspended timber floor, ensure the installer sleeves any airbricks prior to installation and check that they remain unblocked to provide essential ventilation to the timber structure.
> Ask the installer how the holes through which the insulation has been installed will be filled after the work has been completed; poorly skilled installers may leave unsightly blemishes across the face of the wall.
> Resolve any penetrating damp problems before attempting cavity insulation.
> Do not attempt cavity fill if your cavity is less than 50mm.
> Seek impartial advice if your walls are subjected to extreme wind-driven rain conditions as cavity fill may result in damp penetration to the internal wall.
> Avoid polystyrene insulation where there are unprotected PVC cables in the cavity.
> Bear in mind that foam insulation adheres to surrounding masonry and is very difficult to remove so is essentially non-reversible.
> If the cavity fill is poorly executed, it can leave empty pockets which will become thermal bridges, with condensation leading to black mould forming on the internal face.
> Because the outside leaf of the cavity is colder and damper, any metal wall ties may be subjected to accelerated corrosion.

Cavity or solid?

You can tell a lot about a brick wall by looking at its bonding pattern. A cavity wall will have a 'stretcher' bond, where all the bricks are laid with the long side facing outwards. There are usually two skins or leaves of brick joined together with wall ties, typically separated by a 50mm cavity.

As the name implies, solid walls have no cavity, just two or three bricks laid side by side. The wall is generally 9 or 13½ inches (225 or 338mm) and can be identified by end-on or 'header' bricks in the bonding pattern. These are bricks laid at 90 degrees to the wall, keying through to the inside face. The appearance of headers can sometimes be misleading since high-quality modern brickwork may replicate the look of traditional brick bonds using 'snapped' headers – half-bricks in a cavity wall construction.

Left: Stretcher bond in a cavity wall.

Right: Flemish bond with glazed headers in a solid wall.

> Avoid cavity fill if your wall contains an outer leaf of absorbent soft brickwork as this could lead to penetrating damp from rain being absorbed by the cavity insulation.

Lath and plaster linings

In Scotland and parts of northern England, it was common to line the inside face of external walls with a timber studwork frame clad in wooden laths and coated with lime plaster. Lath and plaster was commonly used to form ceilings and internal partitions but here, as an early form of 'dry lining', it continued into the twentieth century. It created a cavity (normally about 50mm) between the external masonry and the inner studwork to give additional insulation. Experimental work is under way to improve the thermal performance of such lined walls with blown insulation materials. Bonded bead and loose cellulose has been shown to give a reasonable reduction in U-value. The techniques are similar to those used for conventional cavity walls.

INSULATING HISTORIC TIMBER FRAMES

With their exposed oak frames and infill panels of wattle and daub or decorative brick, timber-framed buildings are amongst the most energy-inefficient of all traditional building types. Heat loss through the thin walls, coupled with gaps between panel and frame, can create cold and draughty living environments. This makes them a prime target for inappropriate retrofit solutions which trap moisture and leave the frames and wattle panels vulnerable to decay and structural collapse.

Wattle and daub as a material performs well in terms of energy-efficiency due to the large number of air voids trapped within it. But in a timber-framed building the infill panel is generally just 4 inches thick, with a typical U-value of around 2.1 W/m²K. If the infill panels are made of brick, the thermal performance is even worse, approaching a U-value of 2.5 W/m²K.

There are a number of approaches you can take to mitigate the problems of an energy-inefficient timber-frame building. None is simple and they would usually be part of a more extensive programme of repair. Before embarking on any alterations to the external walls, get a condition survey of the structure by an experienced professional and understand how the frame works.

Below left: Loose-fill insulation being blown into the gap between lath and plaster and external wall.

Far left: A timber-framed building with an exposed frame.

Left: Wattle and daub panels are usually hundreds of years old and should be treated with care.

Below left: Modern mastic has been used to close the gaps around the panel and frame, but this has trapped moisture and accelerated decay of the timber.

Airtightness and thermal imaging tests are particularly useful with timber-framed buildings to gain a better understanding of how the building is performing before works commence. Where gaps between panel and frame are wide enough, fill by pushing in breathable quilt, such as hemp, with a knife or screwdriver, and cover it with lime mortar.

External render

Where the timber frame is visible externally, consider applying a lime render right over it. You may be horrified at this suggestion, but there is a good chance that the building was rendered at some point in the past and has been stripped only recently. Look at old photographs from the local record office and study the earlier finishes. Obviously, if the frame is exceptional and was designed to be on show this solution will not be appropriate.

A lime render will not markedly improve the U-value of a timber-framed wall, but it will dramatically reduce draughts from the gaps around the panels while also protecting the frame from further decay. Ensure it is a non-hydraulic lime mix, applied by experienced plasterers used to dealing with such buildings.

The opportunity could be taken to apply an insulated render. Check the breathability of the proposed mix first to ensure that it is compatible with a timber-framed building.

Right: An old photograph (above) shows the thatched timber-framed house with an external lime render. The same house has had the render removed and the frame exposed (below). This will inevitably make it less airtight.

External cladding may be a good option for certain timber-framed buildings in order to improve energy-efficiency, depending on the historic significance of the frame and the local traditions. Weatherboarding or tile-hanging was frequently used in the past; adding either would allow the insertion of insulation material behind, such as a natural quilt. If considering such a solution, always seek professional advice rather than going directly to a tradesman. Such alterations need to be carefully thought through and properly detailed.

Replacement panels

If you have wattle and daub panels, they are likely to be hundreds of years old and their preservation should be paramount. Handmade brick panels became common from the seventeenth century onwards, but frequently, timber-framed buildings contain modern brick or even blockwork panels, with recent plaster finishes. Where the latter applies, consider replacing them with a more compatible material such as hemp and lime. This is the modern equivalent to wattle and daub, and can be cast in-situ to fit the space perfectly. The 'hemp-crete' mixture forms a lightweight concrete-type material, with breathing characteristics that are compatible with the timber frame. It will reduce heat loss by reducing conductivity through the panel and, if carefully detailed, will minimise the gaps between the panels and the frame to improve airtightness. To increase thermal performance this infill can be cast even thicker than the frame, covering the timbers either internally or externally. Adding 100mm of cover over the frame will double the thermal insulation of the wall.

Above: A sixteenth-century timber-framed house following extensive repair and sensitive thermal upgrading. Modern infill panels have been replaced with hemp and lime.

Internal insulation

Where neither the infill panels nor external appearance can be changed, the option is to insulate from the inside. Be aware that timber-framed buildings of any merit dating from the seventeenth century or earlier may contain wall paintings. Often they are found on early plasterwork behind layers of later paint so seek advice and consent if necessary before stripping original plaster. If they are not present or where, as is often the case, modern gypsum plaster has been applied, an insulating substrate, such as reed board with a lime plaster, could be a good solution (➡ Insulating systems, page 113). This provides a little insulation while remaining breathable, thus preventing problems with interstitial condensation or wind-driven rain.

Far left: Hemp and lime is ideal for casting replacement panels in timber frames, particularly in awkward-shaped holes.

Left: Hemp 'shiv' and a lime binder are blended in a mixer. Before the hemp lime has fully cured, remove the shuttering and press back the edges to allow for the thickness of plaster to butt against the side of the frame.

7

Floors

Floors have a big impact on comfort levels in our homes and can result in considerable heat loss. Depending on the construction, it may be possible to upgrade the thermal efficiency of a floor through simple measures. The challenges are to avoid upsetting the building's moisture equilibrium or destroying its historic character.

The ground floors of old houses were generally of either solid or suspended construction. Solid floors consisted of compacted earth often with stone flags, bricks or tiles laid on top. Suspended floors are more sophisticated and were formed of wooden boards nailed to a timber joist structure with ventilation beneath.

Over the last few decades, many old floors have been needlessly removed in a misguided attempt to stop damp through the installation of a concrete slab and damp-proof membrane. Sadly, this has often been disastrous as it has simply exacerbated the damp, causing further damage to the building and resulting in an expensive mistake that is incredibly difficult to reverse.

The quest for energy savings, through improved insulation and airtightness, presents another major threat to surviving old floors and is likely to result in additional unnecessary loss. Before doing anything, understand what you have and look at ways of upgrading the floor to provide a thermally efficient solution using simple techniques that work with the character and breathing structure of the building. In some cases it may be possible to incorporate underfloor heating systems that will enhance your comfort.

BUILDING REGULATIONS

When ground floors are being replaced, they must comply with current U-values for new buildings. If existing floors are thermally upgraded, they are required to meet a less stringent U-value under the circumstances listed in Chapter 2, page 29. Upper floors would not usually require insulation unless they form part of the thermal envelope, for instance a room over an unheated garage.

The regulations accept that compliance may not be possible if this would cause 'significant problems in relation to adjoining floor levels' – i.e. if insulation would raise the level of the floor, resulting in a step at the edges, or the need to trim the bottom of historic doors.

Beautiful old floors at The Landmark Trust's Calverley Old Hall. The flagstone floor to the dining room (opposite) and suspended timber floor to the bedroom (below) add character to the historic setting.

CHARACTER AND BEAUTY

Both solid and suspended floors can have aesthetic and historic value. Stone flags, tiles or bricks rarely look the same when taken up and relaid, and may be damaged in the process. Old floorboards often have a surface patina, or a distinct joint or nail pattern, and may be fragile if disturbed. Think hard before lifting a floor, especially if the boards are very wide or historically valuable, as damage is almost inevitable.

Consider the implications before adding insulation above an existing solid or suspended floor. Such actions will have an impact on period features such as skirtings and staircases, and doors will need to be trimmed. Low electrical sockets will also require adjustment. The overall room height will be affected and, where doors are already low, this may present real problems. If only certain areas are being insulated, the step up can be a trip hazard so a ramp might be necessary. Where character and beauty are compromised it may be better not to insulate.

Above: The floor of the room over this passageway will require additional insulation to prevent excessive heat loss.

Above right: The character of old floors, such as these flagstones, is invariably lost if they are lifted or disturbed.

Right: Any insulation that raises the level of a floor will impact on doors and skirtings.

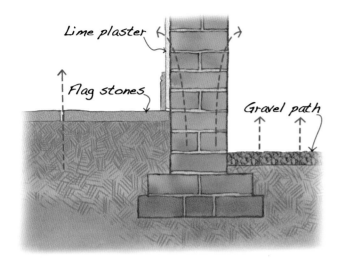

Above: Traditional solid floors do not incorporate a DPM. Any dampness in the earth can easily evaporate through permeable junctions and finishes. The external ground level should be kept below the internal floor level to stop damp tracking across.

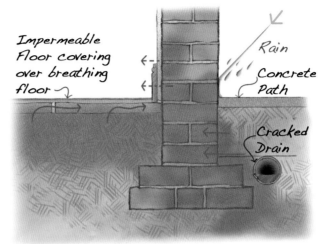

Above: If external ground levels are allowed to rise above the internal floor level, moisture will track across, causing dampness in the floor and the base of the wall and decay to skirtings. Cracked drains may result in localised dampness and concrete paths will prevent evaporation. If impermeable floor coverings are laid, they will cause the floor to sweat.

Below: Coir is an ideal finish for breathing floors.

SOLID FLOORS

Traditional ground floors usually consisted of tiles or flags laid on compacted earth. It was not uncommon to incorporate a bed of sand or lime mortar to level them and prevent them from rocking. By their very nature, these floors were often slightly damp, evaporating a small amount of moisture from the earth below through the gaps in the flags or tiles or through the surface of unglazed bricks. The draughty interior would readily dissipate the moisture, without it causing a problem.

Fitted carpets, rubber-backed underlays, linoleum and vinyl laid on breathable solid floors will trap moisture and cause the floor to 'sweat'. After removing coverings, give the floor an opportunity to dry out as, once allowed to breathe, it may require no further work and can be left undisturbed. If salts become evident during the drying out process they should be vacuumed off (➠ Dealing with flooding, page 172).

If dampness is evident, bear in mind that thermal performance will be compromised and the living environment will be less heathy. Check external ground levels which should always be lower than the internal floor, and keep rainwater gullies unblocked. If damp is still noticed, commission a drainage survey before

Concrete floor slabs

In recent years, 'refurbishment' has usually resulted in old floors being taken up and replaced with a concrete floor slab, usually incorporating a plastic sheet or damp-proof membrane (DPM). While the intention of a DPM has been to prevent damp from rising, it has often simply pushed the moisture from under the floor to the outside walls, creating a rising damp problem. This is frequently misdiagnosed and incorrectly treated when the floor itself shows no sign of failure.

This is even more likely where the floors have been excavated to accommodate the thickness of a concrete slab, or to increase the floor-to-ceiling height within the room. By digging further down, you find earth that often contains more moisture and the problem is exacerbated.

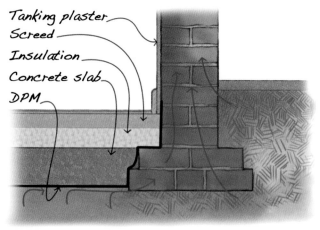

Above: Concrete slabs are often laid to resolve problems with damp floors but, as the DPM under the slab is not linked to a DPC in the wall, they tend to force ground moisture to the edge and create rising damp. Low-level impermeable tanking plasters are often used to mask the problem, but these push the moisture further up the wall, leaving the masonry damp and thermally inefficient.

considering other options. This will indicate whether pipes are passing under or close to the house and will locate any leaks. Old pot drains – the earthenware pipes that preceded modern plastic – are often fractured, concentrating moisture at the base of a wall or under a floor. Also check mains water pipes for potential leaks and soakaways. Before work to a floor starts, remedy any defects or take the opportunity to replace drains and pipework where necessary.

Where an old floor is present, any attempt to lift it, either for damp-proofing or to install insulation or underfloor heating, is extremely inadvisable. It will never look as beautiful or have as much character once it is relaid and the introduction of impermeable layers is likely to upset the moisture equilibrium within the walls of the building and cause low-level damp.

Plaster floors

While concrete floor slabs are often unwelcome in old buildings, take care not to confuse them with plaster floors. In areas where gypsum was readily available, such as the Midlands, plaster floors were commonly laid from late medieval times up to the nineteenth century. They look surprisingly similar to concrete. Tragically they are often destroyed, as their historic value is not recognised.

Until comparatively recently, concrete floor slabs and screeds were laid without any insulation incorporated. Unlike earth, which is an insulator, concrete is a reasonably good conductor so feels cold to the touch. Underlay laid on top and a thick carpet will largely counteract the problem but, where ceramic tiles or stone flags are laid directly on the concrete, the floor will feel particularly cold to walk on in bare feet during the winter months. Intermittent heat sources, which are only

Left: Breaking up and removing a concrete floor is a major undertaking, but may be necessary in instances where it is causing damp in the walls.

Above: Where a concrete floor is not causing dampness, it may be possible to insulate it with a floating wood floor, laid on thin insulating sheet.

switched on for a couple of hours at a time, are rarely adequate to bring such floors up to a comfortable temperature; they may even cause condensation on the cold surface of the floor.

So what can be done with a cold, solid, concrete floor? This remains one of the greatest challenges when upgrading for thermal efficiency. Occasionally, where the concrete was laid several decades ago, it might be of a limited thickness of 40 or 50mm. It may be worth taking this up and starting from scratch. Doing this provides an opportunity to incorporate insulation and underfloor heating within the new floor.

More generally, concrete slabs were laid between 100 and 150mm in thickness and some may have had steel reinforcement included, so removal is a major undertaking, involving heavy machinery and vibration to the building. This level of invasive work may cause more damage than leaving the floor in place.

Assuming the concrete is not pushing damp to the outside walls, it may be worth replacing the cold tiles or flags with a wooden floor, or even a carpet and thermal underlay. Both would act as insulators and provide a degree of thermal comfort underfoot. If there is enough headroom, it may be possible to incorporate a thin insulating layer with electric underfloor heating.

Air leakage with solid floors should not be forgotten. Shrinkage around the edges during the drying process can result in cracks that allow air leakage paths.

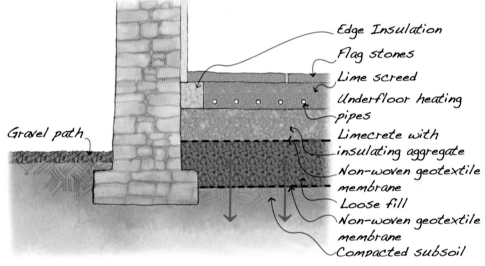

Gravel path

Edge Insulation
Flag stones
Lime screed
Underfloor heating pipes
Limecrete with insulating aggregate
Non-woven geotextile membrane
Loose fill
Non-woven geotextile membrane
Compacted subsoil

Limecrete floors

'Limecrete' is a material similar to concrete. Rather than a mix of cement and aggregate, it consists of hydraulic lime and aggregate, and can be used to make a structural floor slab that is vapour-permeable.

Developed in the late 1990s, limecrete floors have become established as a practical alternative to concrete floor slabs. There are hundreds, if not thousands, in existence across the UK, providing evidence that the system can work well. Limecrete floors are ideal for use where a solid insulated floor is required but where the walls have no physical damp-proof course. In such cases, the installation of a concrete slab and DPM would risk pushing dampness to the walls, resulting in rising damp.

Above: A limecrete floor provides a breathable, insulated alternative to a concrete slab and is more suited to an old building.

Laying limecrete

1. The earth within the building is excavated to a suitable depth, and the ground is levelled. The loose fill is then placed and levelled.

2. If using recycled foam glass (RFG), this will require a light compaction.

3. A non-woven geotextile is placed over the loose fill to contain the limecrete when it is poured. If a radon barrier is necessary, this is laid over the loose fill, but should be avoided if possible.

4. Scaffold tubes are used to set the levels.

5. The limecrete is mixed on site, carefully batched with water added to produce a 'porridge' consistency. It is then poured on to the geotextile.

6. The slab is levelled, in this instance using a scaffold pole as a guide for a straight edge as it is drawn across.

7. The limecrete is floated up, taking care to maintain an accurate level.

Depending on their exact build-up, limecrete floors can be highly insulated, vapour-permeable and may incorporate underfloor heating.

Limecrete floors can be designed to meet the current Building Regulations for U-values. Certain suppliers have established a 'system type approval' with local authority building control departments. This means that a limecrete floor, specified by accredited suppliers, will gain automatic building regulation approval.

Understanding limecrete

In order to meet Building Regulations, limecrete floor systems must provide a barrier to rising ground moisture, as well as adequate insulation. This is achieved using a layer of loose-fill material such as recycled foam glass (RFG) aggregate or lightweight expanded clay aggregate (LECA). This is typically 100–150mm thick, but may vary according to the U–value required. Both aggregates are produced in lumps of 10mm or more across, creating large air voids between. The absence of fine particles in the loose-fill layer prevents moisture from the ground being drawn up via capillary action, hence it acts as a barrier to moisture. If the water level rises within a limecrete floor, it is free to do so within the thickness of the loose fill, and to drain freely when the water recedes without causing damage. It is essential, however, as with all floor systems, that any ground water issues are resolved before the installation of the floor. This could involve the construction of French drains around the building or, in some cases, drainage may be necessary beneath the loose-fill insulation layer.

Once the loose fill is down, a non-woven geotextile membrane is usually laid over the top. This is principally to prevent the limecrete layer above from running down between the loose fill and providing a path for water via capillary action.

The limecrete slab is cast next, mixed on site using hydraulic lime and a well-graded aggregate. For an insulating limecrete slab, a lightweight aggregate is used. Some suppliers have developed their own insulating blended aggregates but, as an alternative, a blend of two grades of LECA can be used. The limecrete slab is the loadbearing element, and is usually cast 100–150mm deep. If a lightweight aggregate is used, the limecrete slab contributes to the insulation value of the floor and would form part of the U-value calculation.

Limecrete: loose fill

The products used in the loose-fill layer of a limecrete floor are aerated, and are therefore good insulators, providing excellent insulation for the floor.

RFG (recycled foam glass) aggregate has a high bearing capacity. It is generally the preferred loose fill as it is irregular in shape and therefore 'locks' together, making it possible to walk on and therefore quicker and easier to lay; it does require a light tamping. This translates into labour cost savings in installation. As well as the structural advantages, this material also has lower thermal conductivity than LECA (lightweight expanded clay aggregate), and can therefore be laid in a slightly thinner layer.

LECA has the advantage of being cheaper, but is manufactured from a quarried product and is fired at a higher temperature, making it less sustainable. It is spherical in form so is more difficult to lay – it is rather like walking on a layer of marbles.

Top: RFG is more angular than LECA.

Above: LECA granules.

Limecrete curing

There is a common misconception that lime takes forever to 'go off'. A limecrete slab can usually bear weight within a day or two of laying, although curing times are largely dependent on temperature and humidity levels on site. As with concrete, it is important to maintain temperatures above 5°C (ideally between 10°C and 18°C) and to have good ventilation to control humidity. That said, in warm dry conditions it will be necessary to dampen down the limecrete for several days to prevent rapid drying before carbonation has had a chance to take place. In general, it is wise to allow between two and three weeks before laying any floor finish or screed layer. This is to give time for the carbonation process, the mechanism by which it gains its strength, and also time for the slab to dry. The total length of drying/curing time necessary will depend on the thickness of the slab and the site conditions.

Limecrete and underfloor heating (UFH)

Where an underfloor heating system is being installed, it is laid on top of the limecrete slab. Steel reinforcement mesh, sometimes used to fix the pipes, is not recommended as it may corrode over time. Alternative methods of fixing UFH pipes include using stainless steel or plastic mesh, clip rails or mechanically fixing to the surface of the limecrete with pipe clips. It is important to maintain vapour-permeability and to avoid plastic tray systems that cover the entire floor, essentially introducing a DPM into your build-up (➡ Underfloor heating, page 153).

A vapour-permeable screed is laid over the heating pipes, usually 50–75mm thick, depending on the thickness of the pipework. If large stone flags are laid on top, a thinner screed may be acceptable as the point-loading is minimised. Screed is made from hydraulic lime and sharp, well-graded aggregate. It has no insulating component so allows heat to pass through without resistance. Edge insulation is usually incorporated around the screed to minimise thermal bridging – although, where low-level damp is apparent, this may not be appropriate.

If underfloor heating is not installed, the screed can be omitted from the build-up and the floor finish can be applied directly to the limecrete slab.

Limecrete floor finishes

The ideal floor finish is stone flag, ceramic tile or brick. These should be laid in, and pointed up with, a hydraulic lime mortar, ideally NHL 3.5 to maintain breathability.

Wooden floors can be used if the floor has fully dried prior to laying boards. These should be laid on battens to maintain an air gap; however, this makes UFH considerably less efficient. Take advice from your flooring supplier about the most appropriate type of wooden floor.

When laying rugs over a limecrete floor, avoid rubber-backed underlays or other non-breathable types. Coir mats are particularly suited as they allow moisture to readily evaporate.

Limecrete and radon

If working within a radon area or where landfill gas is an issue, you may be required to take precautionary measures. A standard radon sump can be fitted, or the loose-

Top: For a fully breathable solution following flood damage, these tiles were cast from hydraulic lime and sand, and laid over a limecrete floor.

Above: Old bricks are bedded over a cast floor slab.

fill layer can be vented to the outside using small pipes passing through the wall, terminated in a suitable grille. If a physical radon barrier is necessary, it can be installed above the loose-fill layer. This will prevent water vapour passing across but the loose fill will still act as a moisture-buffer, allowing ground water to rise and fall within it. For advice, speak to a limecrete supplier and consult your building control officer.

Limecrete: key issues

> Mixing limecrete is a major undertaking, as it does not arrive on site ready-mixed like concrete. For a small floor, two standard bell- or drum-mixers may suffice, but for larger areas a paddle mixer may be necessary. These can be hired relatively easily.

> A limecrete floor typically has a 200–500mm build-up. If digging down to accommodate this thickness, be careful not to undermine the footings of the building. Dig a trial hole to establish the depth of the existing wall and, if in doubt, consult a structural engineer.

> Establish the level of the water table by digging a trial hole before excavating down to lay a floor. Although moisture can freely rise and fall within the loose-fill layer, the water table must not reach the limecrete slab as it has high capillarity and will absorb moisture.

> Make sure that the top of the loose-fill layer is above the external ground level, otherwise ground moisture may track across and create dampness within the limecrete layer.

Floors and U-values

Solid-ground floors bearing on to the earth lose heat at a much slower rate than other thermal elements such as walls and roofs. Earth is a reasonable insulator, and therefore resists heat flow through the floor construction. In addition, flags or tiles have high thermal mass, storing heat and re-releasing it, resulting in a surface temperature that is surprisingly warm if the house is heated.

As the floor is usually above external ground level, a thermal bridge exists around the edge of the room where heat flows through the external walls, cooling the floor at the perimeter.

This means that solid-floor U-values cannot be calculated simply by looking at the detail and thickness of the construction materials. The heat loss takes into account the exposed perimeter, the length of floor abutting an external wall. Most companies offering floor insulation products provide a free U-value calculator, whereby specific details of the project are entered and the heat loss is calculated, along with the necessary thickness of a particular insulation product to meet Building Regulations.

U-values of suspended timber floors are easier to calculate, as the heat is lost to the ventilated cavity beneath.

Below: U-values to floors take account of the exposed perimeter.

Carpets and underlays

Thick wall-to-wall fitted carpets and thermal underlays are the easiest means of insulating suspended floors or modern concrete floors that have a damp-proof membrane. A number of environmentally friendly products produced from recycled, natural materials are available. With suspended floors, laying hardboard first will improve airtightness. Where underfloor heating is installed, carpets and underlays will reduce the heat output and, when laid on solid floors, they separate the thermal mass of the floor from the room. If sound insulation is an issue, ask about acoustic underlays.

Left: Lifting floor coverings to expose wooden boards can create cold and draughty interiors, and also reduce acoustic insulation between traditional wooden floor structures.

SUSPENDED TIMBER FLOORS

When there was no cellar beneath, suspended floors were normally constructed by building a series of parallel 'sleeper' walls to carry joists at ground-floor level. These were just a few courses high, built of honey-comb bonded brick which allowed air to circulate. Grilles were fitted externally at low level on opposite walls to draw ventilation through, preventing the build-up of moist air which would rot the timber.

The drawback of ventilation under suspended floors was that the air flow caused a draught within the room which had a dramatic effect on room temperature. The problem was exacerbated because, as the boards seasoned and shrank, gaps occurred between them. As sawmill technology developed, the tongue-and-groove floorboard appeared. The tongue bridged the gap between the boards so, even when the boards shrank, the draught was greatly reduced.

Above right: Suspended timber ground-floor construction.

Above centre: Ventilation grille for a suspended timber floor. This example also shows a slate damp-proof course.

Right: A typical 4 x 4m room has approximately 27 floorboards. If there is a 1mm gap between each, the approximate total gap area is 0.1m² – equivalent to leaving a small window permanently open.

Draughtproofing

Ensuring a suspended timber floor is as airtight as possible has a considerable impact on heat loss and can be achieved relatively easily and cheaply.

Suspended timber floors can be made far less draughty simply by blocking up the air grilles on the outside walls. Unfortunately, this shuts off the source of ventilation, and may cause the floor structure to decay, so alternative forms of draught management are required. For a simple and non-invasive solution, timber floors can be draughtproofed using a variety of proprietary draught strip systems.

Whatever you decide to use, particular attention should be paid to the gap at the bottom of the skirting board around the edges of the room where the draughts will often be greatest. If fitting a carpet, make sure this is addressed before the fitters arrive as it will not be possible afterwards. If it is left, it will cause the edges of the carpet to attract dirt and moth.

If the gap is large enough, use a screwdriver to push in a foam strip – this will stop the draught and minimise the thermal bridge. Expanding foam is sometimes used in larger gaps but is notoriously difficult to control and tends to disappear into the void, so experiment first.

More often, the gap is only 2 or 3mm and may need a bead of silicone mastic carefully applied with a mastic gun. Choose a product with a thin nozzle and push it as far as possible into the gap to fill the thickness of the space, then run your finger over the joint for a neat finish. A continuous bead should be just enough to stop the draught, but it may be broken if the skirting boards shrink.

For a more traditional option, gaps between floorboards and skirting boards can be filled with thin slivers of matching timber. Stained balsa wood is sometimes used as it can be compressed into the gaps. Alternatively, stain lengths of string – or even sash cord for wider gaps – to match the colour of the boards and then, like caulking the deck of a ship, glue and push the string into place. Be sure to wipe off the glue as you work to prevent it marking the timber. Where floors are particularly delicate or historic, papier-mâché may be the most appropriate solution for filling gaps.

Suspended upper floors do not generally need draughtproofing or insulating, except where they bridge unheated spaces – for example, above garages and external passageways.

Top: For larger gaps, specially designed foam strips are available which can be compressed and forced into the gap where they expand to fit tightly in place.

Above: For smaller gaps, up to around 5mm, a 'V'-profile strip made from a flexible plastic can be pushed into the gaps and, in theory, will spring open and stay in position.

Right: Insulation has been laid between these joists, but unless airtightness has also been addressed, it is unlikely to be particularly effective.

Insulation

Even where draughts are minimised or eliminated, the heat loss through a timber floor with a ventilated sub-floor void is considerable. Effective insulation requires access to the space between the joists. Where there is an unheated cellar below, or a crawl space of 900mm or more, the job can usually be tackled from underneath and is relatively straightforward. If only a shallow void exists, the boards will need to be lifted; this should be done with care and is not always advisable.

Very often old boards split in the process of lifting. If boards are tongue-and-grooved it is extremely difficult to lift them without snapping off the tongue when levering them up. If they are relaid without the tongue, their appearance will be ruined and the benefit of sub-floor insulation reduced by the increase in draughts. Early boards which were not produced in a sawmill, and therefore are of varying thickness, were painstakingly shaped on their reverse to fit over the joist and sit flush on the upper surface. Each board therefore has a specific location, making it extremely difficult to relay.

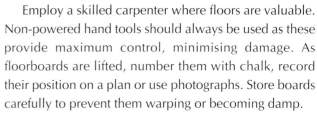

Above: Floorboards were usually fixed with special 'cut' nails which were designed to grip into the joist and reduce squeaks, making the boards particularly difficult to lever up. In high-quality floors, 'secret' nailing was often used into the edges of the boards, making removal even more difficult.

Left: Old elm boards such as these are fragile and difficult to replace.

Below left: Not all floorboards will survive being lifted. Think twice before disturbing old boards, particularly if they are elm.

Employ a skilled carpenter where floors are valuable. Non-powered hand tools should always be used as these provide maximum control, minimising damage. As floorboards are lifted, number them with chalk, record their position on a plan or use photographs. Store boards carefully to prevent them warping or becoming damp.

Skirting boards may also have to be removed, resulting in further disruption. Where floorboards are lifted, always check thoroughly for damp and beetle infestation and deal with the causes as well as the symptoms.

If boards are likely to be taken up again in the future, or where they are above fragile ceilings, screw them down with slotted (rather than cross-headed) brass screws as opposed to nailing them down.

Before lifting old floorboards, always consider:

> Are the boards of particular character and age? Are the boards tongue-and-grooved? If so, lifting may best be avoided.
> Are the boards in good condition? If not, replacement may be inevitable, and insulation should be incorporated at the same time.
> Is the sub-floor structure in good condition? Sometimes earth and debris build up under a suspended floor structure, blocking ventilation and causing decay. Try lifting an individual floorboard or use a boroscope to check condition.
> If the floor bounces when walked on, it may require more extensive repair and strengthening to the structure.
> Beware of lifting the entire floor at once as this can destabilise the joists and sleeper walls.

Insulation from above

If floorboards are easy to lift and are of no historic merit, or when the floor structure requires repair, insulation between the joists is worth considering. While boards are lifted, take the opportunity to remove any debris from the under-floor void to increase ventilation.

Due to its superior k-value, foil-faced foam board provides the highest level of insulation between joists. Wood fibreboard can be used in the same way and, although its insulation value is not as good, it has hygroscopic properties that will assist in moisture-buffering where relative humidity is an issue.

When fitting rigid board insulation, care is required to avoid gaps around the edges as this will compromise

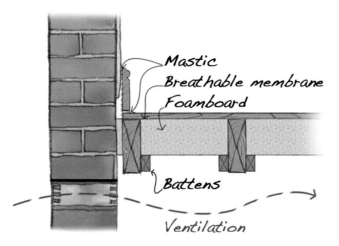

Above: Where foam boards or wood fibreboards are used between joists, ensure they are cut accurately for a snug fit. A strip of breathable membrane can be used to lap around the perimeter to improve airtightness. Where the gap is wide enough, insulate between the joist and wall.

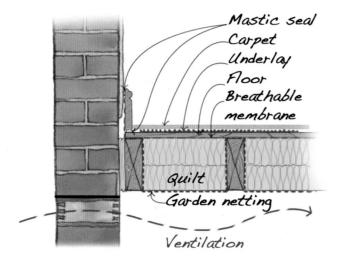

Above: Quilt or batts can be used between joists, supported in a trough formed from plastic garden netting. A breathable membrane can be laid over the top to improve airtightness.

Right: An alternative method to garden netting (see diagram below left) is to form the troughs from a breathable membrane. This will also form an airtight barrier but, because this material is quite stiff, it can be tricky to fold at the ends of the troughs in a way that minimises air leakage.

Below right: Another option when insulating from above is the use of cellulose insulation, contained within troughs made of breathable membrane.

airtightness. They also need to be adequately secured to stop them dropping down between the joists. This is achieved by screwing thin wooden battens to their sides. The top of the insulation should be level with the top of the joist to minimise the air void between the insulation and the underside of the floorboard.

Another technique is to use quilt or batts between the joists. The simplest method of doing this is to run garden netting over the joists, hanging down to form troughs in between. These are filled with quilt insulation to the desired thickness. To create an airtight barrier, a breathable membrane, lapped up and fixed behind the skirting, can be laid above the joists before the boards are relaid. This may, however, be problematic on exposed floorboards where water is frequently spilt, for instance bathrooms. In such instances the liquid will run through the gaps between the floorboards and sit on the membrane with nowhere to go, potentially rotting the timber from beneath.

Wood fibreboard over floors

Where the finished floor level is not restricted, a floating floor of tongue-and-groove wood fibreboard laid over the joists, with floorboards on top, is an option. This combines thermal insulation with airtightness and, unlike foam board, provides good acoustic insulation, making it ideal for use between flats. It also has the major advantage over foam board of a much higher compressive strength, making it suitable for this application where foam board would not be.

Insulation from below

If access is available from below, either from a cellar or an adequate crawl space under the building, the task of insulating a suspended floor is far more straightforward. Fix quilt or foam board between the joists, pushing it up to fill any gap between the top of the insulation and the underside of the floorboards; a quilt should fill the full depth of the joist; a rigid board can be secured in position with screws.

Once insulated, fit an airtight layer to the underside of the joists. For example, tongue-and-groove wood fibreboard will provide additional thermal and acoustic insulation. If the product selected is not fire-rated, finish with two layers of plasterboard with staggered junctions where necessary.

Left: Where access is available from below, floors can be insulated without disturbing boards.

UNDERFLOOR HEATING

Electric and wet (hydronic) underfloor heating (UFH) systems are available, with options for both solid and suspended timber flooring. Wet systems employ loops of pipe while electric systems use heating cables or mats. As the systems offered by different manufactures vary greatly in the way they are installed, it is important to decide which is the most appropriate for each application and to balance efficiency with the potential impact it may have on the breathability and fabric of the building.

To prevent heat flowing into the walls and sub-floor it is essential that the perimeter and underside of the heated floor is well insulated.

Solid floors

With solid floors, the UFH cables or pipes are generally fixed to the floor insulation and a concrete or lime screed is laid over them. The floor finish is then laid over this. Alternatively, electric heating mats may be laid directly over existing floors below new tiled surfaces.

Suspended timber floors

The heat output achieved with suspended timber floors is likely to be lower than with solid floors. With wet systems, a variety of installation methods are used. One way of achieving good performance is to fix the UFH pipes on to insulated boards fixed between the joists and to embed the pipes in a sand-and-cement 'screed' poured over them. Floorboards or other finishes can then be laid in the conventional way. The downside of this system is the weight of the screed, especially at upper floor levels.

Alternative methods involve installing emission plates or panels between the joists and installing the pipes into them. In some instances, when UFH is installed on upper floors, the pipes are simply installed between the joists with reflective foil and insulation beneath them.

Electric heating cables are also suitable for suspended timber floors. It is essential to follow the manufacturer's directions and to ensure that the correct insulation method is used to prevent overheating.

Paints

Paints and other finishes are an easily overlooked part of the sustainability jigsaw. Their principal purpose is to enhance and protect. Less positively, their manufacture has the potential to be environmentally damaging and their use can impact both on human health and old buildings that need to breathe.

Appropriately used, paints and other finishes help to maintain and extend the life of materials, saving wasteful replacement and, as a result, the use of natural resources and energy. Inappropriate use can prove disastrous, leading to damp and decay.

When choosing a paint or finish, especially for exterior use, the priority should be for it to have a long-lasting finish but this must be balanced by the need for it to work in sympathy with the building and its occupants. The least ecological product of all is one which fails to work, or results in problems that lead to the loss of a building's fabric, or makes the people using it or living with it unwell.

There is a vast range of coatings available and evaluating them is a hugely complicated and sometimes emotive subject. Even specialist chemists find it hard to agree on what constitutes an environmentally friendly product, and product information is often misleading. It is extremely difficult to create a coating which is going to provide good durability, coverage and ease of application without some environmental consequences. What is certain is that some so-called eco, green, natural or organic paint products are far more virtuous than others.

THE PURPOSE OF PAINTS

Paint technology has come a very long way since the days of simple limewashes and distempers. Those paints were made from materials that were readily available, and were often mixed up on site and applied as part of an ongoing maintenance cycle. Limewash was used annually on buildings associated with animals, to exploit its alkalinity as a means of killing germs. Patented paint formulations started to appear from the nineteenth century and 'washable or sanitary distemper' was developed as a more durable finish to soft distemper in response to growing hygiene standards.

Today, paint and other finishes protect surfaces from the damaging effects of moisture, ultra-violet (UV) light, atmospheric pollution and general wear and tear, and make cleaning easier. Paints are developed with perma-

Opposite: As well as providing essential protection, paints add individuality to houses.

Below: Some substrates require vapour-permeable paints to allow the wall to breathe, such as this limewash to a rubble-stone house in Wales.

The problem with 'modern' paints

There is a common misconception that to keep moisture out of an old wall a waterproof paint has to be used. Yet old buildings move; they expand and contract, and are subject to seasonal movement due to their shallow foundations, causing hairline cracks in structure, render and paint finishes. The waterproof nature of modern paints causes rain to run off wall surfaces without being absorbed but, when water finds a crack, it is concentrated and sucked in through capillary action. Once it has penetrated the waterproof paint layer, it is absorbed and dispersed and unable to escape. In addition, any residual moisture in the core or water vapour passing through the breathing wall is also trapped by waterproof paints. Depending on the situation, transparent waterproofing treatments to brickwork and stonework perform in much the same way, potentially trapping damp within rather than keeping it out, so are therefore best avoided.

Above: Colour can dramatically alter the appearance of a building, but choosing the right type of paint is essential.

Above right: The masonry paint on this rubble-stone cottage was trapping damp (left). It was removed using 'scutch' hammers, repointed in non-hydraulic lime and limewashed, allowing it to breathe (right).

nence, durability and flexibility in mind as well as ease of use, yet there is often a trade-off between durability and breathability.

Paint formulations for wood are generally different from those developed for plaster and masonry, and most paints are designed for either interior or exterior use. Other specialist paints are available for almost any substrate; there is even a paint for coating PVCu windows that have yellowed over time. Yet with all these clever scientific advances, when it comes to old buildings there is a general move back to simple paints in subtle shades that allow our homes to breathe.

Breathable versus waterproof

It may seem counter-intuitive, but the best way of keeping a wall dry is to coat it in a breathable paint. In theory, breathable paints have a degree of vapour-permeability, allowing moisture vapour to pass through them and preventing it from building up in the core of the wall. This is advantageous in many situations but particularly when used on solid-walled, traditional constructions where the unimpeded passage of vapour is crucial to the longevity of the building.

Some breathable paints also have high capillarity, or capillary openness. This means they are able to absorb water as a liquid. Traditional paints such as limewash, casein and distemper come into this category, and are

Left: If paint darkens as it gets wet, it is not only highly breathable but 'capillary-open', and able to absorb liquid water.

easily identified by their darkening in colour when they get wet. By absorbing water on contact, they prevent the gushing effect of rain down a wall which would otherwise leave cracks in surfaces vulnerable to concentrated water penetration.

While some capillary-open paints are ideal for evaporating large quantities of water, they are not always suited to exposed situations where rain may penetrate deep into the wall if unimpeded. For this reason, most modern breathable paint formulations, such as silicate-based paints, contain hydrophobic additives to stop liquid water, or rain, from passing through them. Such paints are highly vapour-open while remaining capillary-closed. The tradition of adding tallow or linseed oil to limewash developed due to the desire to make the coating shed water in a similar fashion but, unlike hydrophobic additives, these also block the passage of water vapour and can trap moisture. For this reason, they are best avoided, except on surfaces where rapid water run-off is desirable, such as painted external cills or coping stones.

What is particularly concerning is the vast number of paints that claim to be breathable but are neither capillary-open, nor vapour-permeable. As breathability is a relative concept, which is not quantified, manufacturers are producing paints which are marginally less waterproof than their forerunners and marketing them as breathable when, in practice, they are not.

Matt or gloss?

There is a compromise to be made when choosing a paint for an old building. Matt finishes are generally more breathable but are not as durable as paints with some degree of sheen or gloss. Anyone with young children will appreciate the vulnerability of paint finishes, when faced with sticky fingers and boisterous play. Also surfaces that receive extra traffic and are regularly touched, such as stairwells and hallways or around light switches, will deteriorate quicker if decorated with a completely matt paint such as soft distemper. Conversely, paints with a gloss finish are usually highly impermeable, but are generally the most durable. Therefore gloss paint may be very practical on a skirting board, which is subjected to knocks from the vacuum cleaner, but potentially disastrous on a breathing wall. Oil-based gloss paints tend to be more durable than water-based (acrylic) paints.

Below: Paints are available in matt or gloss, but have different levels of durability.

The myth of microporous

Many paints designed for joinery are branded as 'micro-porous' although this is, strictly speaking, a misnomer: a material can contain pores, but unless these are linked, they will not allow the passage of water vapour and will have no bearing on vapour-permeability (➡ Porosity and vapour-permeability, page 44). In reality, a microporous paint may have little or no capacity to breathe. The term was invented in the 1980s and used for marketing purposes, but has never been scientifically defined.

Paint and wood

Paint systems for joinery, such as windows and doors, are more complex. Wood swells and contracts according to its moisture content, so any paint finish must be flexible enough to accommodate this move-ment without cracking. Cracks in timber, particularly flat surfaces like window cills, will allow water to penetrate and rot the timber. Blistering is another common paint failure, caused by moisture in the timber trying to escape but being prevented by a waterproof paint. Vapour-permeable paints have been developed for joinery so that any residual moisture in the timber can escape. Yet it is argued that they may do more harm than good in certain situations where there are large fluctuations in relative humidity. As well as letting vapour out, they will also allow water vapour in, causing timber to swell and windows and doors to stick. In such instances, it may be preferable to use a waterproof finish and ensure the wood is dry before application. Ideally, external joinery should only be redecorated following a clear couple of weeks of dry warm weather which has reduced the moisture content of the timber to a sensible level. In reality this may be impossible.

Above: Always choose an appropriate paint for a particular application.

Above right: Paints branded as 'microporous' are misleading.

UNDERSTANDING PAINTS

Modern paints are more complex than traditional formu-lations but all are generally composed of binder, solvent and pigment. The binder, or vehicle, is the most crucial part and is the 'film former', creating a thin layer which adheres to the substrate. Typical binders in traditional paints are glue size in soft distemper, and linseed oil in traditional oil paints. Binders in modern paints include alkyds and acrylics.

The solvent dissolves the binder and thins it to control the viscosity of the paint. Water is the solvent in a water-based paint such as a modern acrylic paint. Oil-based paints contain organic solvents such as alcohol or white spirit. In all paint systems, the drying process includes the evaporation of the solvent, hence oil-based paints have a strong smell for several days after they have been applied. Ideally, rooms should be vacated while this 'off-gassing' is taking place. The same solvent is usually used to wash brushes after use.

Pigments give paint colour. They are ground to a fine powder, but are distinguished from dyes as they are insoluble. White is the most important pigment and is present in most paints, controlling the intensity of the colour and providing opacity; it is needed even with dark colours to avoid translucence. Traditionally, white lead was used. Today, titanium dioxide (TiO_2) is the most widely adopted white pigment in paints because of its high opacity and brilliant whiteness, minimising the number of coats required to achieve coverage.

Often fillers are used to bulk out and thicken the paint and improve the texture. These are usually inert materials such as talc. Complex modern paints contain a variety of other additives and, by combining all these ingredients in appropriate proportions, the required colour, coverage or opacity, thickness, flow, uniformity and drying characteristics are achieved.

MINIMISING THE IMPACT OF DECORATING

Decorating is regarded by many as a simple matter of picking a colour and slapping it on the wall. Yet the choice of paint needs careful consideration, particularly in an old house, if it is to be sustainable for the building and the environment.

Although there is a move towards non-petrochemical based products, all paint has an environmental impact. For some it is much greater than others. Unravelling the true nature of a coating's eco credentials can be far from straightforward. Although many of the factors that need to be assessed to determine the suitability of a product, such as the method of production, distribution and use, are little different from other materials in sustainability terms, the ingredients and performance characteristics are diverse and frequently complex.

Functionality and performance are essential. Paints and finishes that need many coats or frequent reapplication inevitably mean more product is used. This may require the cleaning off or removal of previous coats, possibly resulting in the use of hot air guns or chemical strippers.

Colour choice

A huge range of pigments is now available, making it possible to mix virtually any colour. But originally choice was extremely limited. The earliest colours were provided by earth pigments, such as ochres, umbers and siennas, producing a range of yellows, browns and reds. Still available today, these are natural inorganic pigments and were simply dug from the earth and then ground to a powder; now they are often mined and processed. Earth pigments are relatively cheap and colour-fast, and are ideal for tinting many types of paints. Most traditional limewashes are based on this colour palette.

Right: Natural clays dug from the earth provided the earliest colours.

Below: The range of colours available is now virtually limitless.

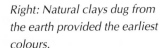

The search for a wider range of colours during the Industrial Revolution brought about a wide diversity of synthetic inorganic pigments, such as Prussian Blue, which are made by mixing and processing a variety of naturally occurring ingredients.

Confusingly, synthetic organic pigments are generally derived from non-sustainable petrochemicals. These colours are often brighter and stronger than their inorganic equivalents and can have good fading resistance, but they lack the subtleties required for a more period palette.

Above left: To save on waste, test a small quantity of paint before committing to buying a large tin.

These factors must balance with the health of the building fabric, the health of the environment and the health of the people applying the coating and occupying the building. In many cases the products used with old buildings will need to be breathable. From the environmental perspective, longevity, renewability, recyclability and biodegradability must all be considered.

The single most environmentally damaging component of paint, beside the various solvents used, is titanium dioxide. Although an abundant natural element, it is not easily accessible and needs a great deal of purifi-

Left: The texture of these wattle and daub panels are so appealing, the home-owner opted to leave them undecorated.

Why paints fail

The principal reasons for failure in paint relate to the expansion and contraction of the material to which they have been applied, the trapping of moisture, the deterioration of the underlying material, UV degradation due to solar radiation or poor surface preparation. As a result, paints may crack, flake, peel, blister or lose their colour. Always choose a paint and compatible primer suitable for the application. Ensure surfaces are dry and dust-free and read manufacturer's instructions carefully. For true sustainability when redecorating, aim to maximise the life of the paint layer as well as protecting the surface beneath.

Left: Masonry paint applied to a damp wall can become detached.

Right: Paint finishes to joinery rely on careful preparation and are vulnerable to expansion and contraction of the substrate.

cation so its production has a significant impact when it comes to the use of resources, energy, habitat loss and waste. But there are few effective alternatives. With pigments, it is generally worth noting that not all natural colours are as eco as they may appear. For example, the production of natural red oxide involves the red ochre pigment being mined, washed, burnt and crushed.

Solvents are equally complicated. Organic solvents are dangerous both as producers of volatile organic compounds (VOCs) and because they can be serious irritants to skin and are generally considered to be more environmentally damaging than those that are water-based. Even so, certain natural solvents such as citrus oil and turpentine are increasingly restricted because of concerns over health. For the same reason most manu-facturers are reviewing the use of preservatives and biocides as well as surfactants and phthalates which are thought to be hormone disrupters.

VOCs in paints

Volatile organic compounds – chemical compounds that vaporise – are found in many building materials. Paints, finishes, thinners and brush-cleaning products tend to be among the most high-profile contributors to problems associated with VOCs. They can affect decorators using the products and those who occupy a building because the 'off-gassing' continues even after a coating has been applied.

Organic solvents are the main, though not the exclusive, source of VOCs in paints. A smell indicates that VOCs are present, and these can come from a variety of sources. For example, rather than a synthetic solvent such as white spirit, some paints contain an orange oil-based solvent with a typical citrus odour. Very few proprietary paints are totally free of VOCs and low-odour paints do not necessarily have low levels of VOCs.

VOC levels are being reduced. By law, manufacturers of all types of paint have been forced to change their formulations to reduce the VOC content of their products. Regulations were originally introduced in 2007 to minimise, monitor and control the harmful effects of VOC content. New, further reduced, VOC limits were introduced from 1 January 2010 and paints must be compliant in formulation and labelling.

SURFACE PREPARATION

Paints and finishes are only as good as the substrate to which they are applied and for this reason manufacturers often recommend removing all previous paint layers. At the very least, peeling and flaking paint must be removed, but many sound traditional finishes can be left undisturbed. Any attempt to remove them will involve releasing toxins into the environment, so always think whether such work is really necessary.

If applying a breathable paint, for instance a limewash, it is necessary to remove any modern, impermeable paints first. This is done for two reasons. First, limewash will not stick to modern paint and, secondly, the wall will not benefit from the breathable quality of the limewash if the modern paint remains.

Defective plaster and rotten timber should be made good and all damp problems resolved. Wherever possible use natural, breathable fillers. When using primers ensure they are suitable for use with subsequent coats.

Above: For a more environmentally friendly option, look for low VOC content in paints.

Top right: Time spent preparing the surface will increase the longevity of the paint finish.

Above right: This early wall-painting was exposed while preparing walls for redecorating.

Remember that in removing paint layers you are destroying the decorative schemes that have gone before, so always leave sound historic layers and simply paint over the top. If you are removing old paint layers or wallpapers, keep fragments and record their position as part of the history of your home. If you have a house predating the eighteenth century it may contain wall-paintings under later coatings. If you spot early fragments of different colours and suspect you may have a wall painting, contact a paint conservator before going any further.

Paint removal

If paint needs to be stripped, consider the product you use. Many traditional chemical paint-removers give off fumes and are irritating to exposed skin. They can also be damaging if they make their way into water courses, so responsible disposal is crucial. A number of solvent-free water-based paint- and varnish-removers are now available which do not cause skin burns or give off harmful odours or fumes and are readily biodegradable.

If stripping impermeable paint finishes from old lime plaster, try using a wallpaper steamer to soften and lift the paint before gently scraping it off with a wide blade.

Above: Check the eco credentials of your paint – not all are what they say on the tin.

Above: A chemical is applied to react with and soften the old paint.

Above: After a specified 'dwell time', a scraper is used to remove the paint. This rarely removes all the paint in a single application.

PAINT TYPES

Traditional finishes such as limewash, casein paints, distempers and linseed oil paints are all, in effect, eco paints. Today, they have been joined by paints branded as 'eco' from a wide range of manufacturers, but it is important to understand the true nature of these paints. Crucially, it is vital to differentiate between mainstream paints, which have had their formulas changed to meet stricter regulations and give the appearance of being green, and those that are truly environmentally friendly and offer a real alternative to products made from petro-chemical derivatives.

True eco paints are far more likely to meet the needs of older buildings. They have high vapour-permeability compared to modern, so called breathable or micro-porous paints. They are made using all or predominantly

Safety

When preparing surfaces for painting always take sensible precautions:
> Wear a good-quality mask when sanding or stripping surfaces and when mixing paints supplied in powder form. Use wet-and-dry paper rather than sandpaper.
> Protect eyes with goggles when sanding or stripping surfaces, including stripping wallpaper, especially where it has been painted.
> Wash solvents and paints off skin promptly, but never use solvents such as white spirit.
> Use ear protectors when mechanically sanding.
> Open windows when burning off paint with hot-air guns and when using paints or solvents that give off fumes.
> Understand the dangers of lead paint and take appropriate precautions.
> Be aware of the risk of fire when using hot-air guns especially near areas where dust may be lodged such as in sash boxes. Stop any 'hot works', such as the use of heat guns, at least one hour before leaving the site and make sure the area is thoroughly checked prior to locking up.
> Never use blow-lamps for paint removal.
> Take great care when working off ladders and platforms and do not overreach.
> Be particularly mindful of dust and fumes if children are living in the house while work is undertaken.

Above: Always wear appropriate safety equipment.

Below: Casein paints give a beautiful texture and are extremely eco, but lack durability.

Bottom: Clay paints have a similar texture to distemper but are much easier to use.

Below right: Contract emulsions, while not particularly green, are usually preferable to vinyl emulsions.

renewable natural materials and are designed to be as non-toxic as possible. Some brands supply their paints in recyclable containers and packaging. Most have little or no smell.

These paints vary from brand to brand and are generally relatively easy to use, although more care is needed than with conventional products especially when it comes to application – some show brush and roller marks more than mainstream products. There are also differences with drying times: eco paints generally take longer to dry than conventional paints so it means that you need to think more carefully about scheduling your project.

Casein or milk paint

Useful for: internal wall and wood surfaces

Consisting principally of casein (a milk protein) and lime, casein paints provide a soft matt finish and can be applied to most internal surfaces. They have a beautiful texture but they lack durability so are not practical for all areas; they are not recommended for use on windows or doors, for example, as they cannot be wiped clean or resist knocks. They often come in powder form and have to be mixed with water and pigments. They are highly breathable, but are not suitable for damp walls or humid rooms such as kitchens or bathrooms as the surface will be susceptible to mould growth. Casein paints do not generally contain titanium dioxide and are free of VOCs, acrylics, oils and solvents.

Clay paint

Useful for: internal wall surfaces

Offering a greener alternative to emulsions, clay paints provide a soft matt finish, are suitable for most interior substrates and come ready-mixed. They have excellent coverage, often requiring only one coat, provide good durability and are available free of odours, VOCs, acrylics and oils; some are free of titanium dioxide. Clay paints are ideal for new or old lime plaster but can also be applied over modern paints or gypsum plasters. Certain clay paints are self-coloured by their natural mineral content.

Clay paints are vapour-permeable and capillary-open, allowing surfaces to breathe and absorb moisture. This helps to regulate the internal humidity of the building and makes them ideal where condensation is a problem, but they should not be used on damp walls.

Contract emulsion

Useful for: internal walls and ceilings

The term emulsion refers to a suspension of tiny droplets of one liquid in a second liquid that ordinarily do not mix together; in this case, tiny drops of vinyl (a petrochemical material) in water. This produces a gel-like consistency in which a pigment can be suspended. Emulsions took over from washable distempers in the mid-twentieth century. Standard, modern emulsions have either vinyl or acrylic resin added to make them more hardwearing and wipeable. However, this also makes them considerably less vapour-permeable.

Trade paint suppliers stock 'contract emulsions' which contain no vinyl. These are designed to be applied as a base coat to new gypsum plaster that has

not fully dried out, to speed up the construction process. While contract emulsions are not as durable as their vinyl counterparts, they serve a useful purpose in old buildings as they allow some degree of water vapour to pass through, making them far more suitable for solid walls. Their lack of vinyl gives them a completely matt finish which is often more in keeping with a period aesthetic. Contract emulsions do contain biocides, surfactants and coalescing agents, as do other standard emulsions.

Above: Lead paint crazes over time, leaving a distinctive and beautiful patina.

Lead paint

Useful for: external timber

Although potentially toxic, lead paint is breathable, flexible, offers unrivalled durability on timber and has an attractive texture and mellow appearance. Compared with modern oil paints it emits fewer VOCs. It is composed of lead pigment – usually lead carbonate ('white lead') – bound in oil and can be tinted with colour. In recent years lead paint has been banned except for use on certain listed buildings. Due to the restrictions imposed on manufacturers most, if not all, are running down their stock and have stopped producing further supplies.

Dealing with old lead paint

Always consider whether lead paint is present before doing anything that may disturb it. Lead was present in many paints applied prior to 1970; it can be confirmed by specialist analysis or by using a DIY test kit. When sanding down old joinery, the presence of lead should be assumed and necessary precautions should be taken; obtain comprehensive information on how to go about the process. Remember:

> The main health risk occurs when lead compounds are ingested or inhaled due to unsound or disturbed paint.
> Children and pregnant women are particularly vulnerable to lead poisoning.
> Dust is the greatest hazard, especially from the inappropriate sanding of old lead paint during its removal or redecoration.
> It may be safer to renew or overcoat lead paint than attempt its removal.
> Because it tends to erode rather than peel, surface preparation may require little more than washing with sugar soap. Only loose paint needs scraping off.
> Where necessary, a light rubbing down using wet (not dry) abrasive paper or chemical strippers may be the solution. Never use hot-air guns due to the fumes that are released.
> The presence of lead paint does not justify stripping historic joinery.

Limewash

Useful for: breathable external wall surfaces

The ultimate eco paint and the most breathable coating available, limewash is basically lime putty (calcium hydroxide) and water. It reabsorbs carbon dioxide, 'carbonates', as it dries and provides a breathable, solvent-free, decorative matt finish.

Limewash is ideal when applied to lime or clay plasters and renders and soft brick or stone. It can also be applied externally to softwood weatherboarding or weathered oak on timber-framed houses. It requires a degree of suction (capillarity) in the substrate in order to stick. To test the suitability of a background, try splashing some water on and observe how quickly it is absorbed. For surfaces where the water runs off, such as cement renders, hard stones such as granite and dense bricks, limewash is less successful as it is unable to key with the substrate. It is not suitable for plasterboard or gypsum plasters and will not adhere to modern impermeable paints such as emulsions and masonry paint.

Limewash is usually applied in up to five thin layers. Due to its watery nature, messy application and the number of coats required, it may not be the first choice for internal application, particularly on ceilings, although some people prefer the aesthetic of limewash and are prepared to put up with its peculiarities. It can be very useful on internal walls that are drying out as its breathability remains unrivalled and most other paints would blister or flake in that situation. When used externally, it typically needs renewing every four to five years but this is dependent on the suction of the substrate and the exposure of the building. For a rough rule of thumb each coat of limewash will give one year's protection.

Left: Rather than flaking like most modern paints, lead paint often remains sound and can be overcoated rather than stripped back to bare wood.

Right: Limewash should be applied to a dampened substrate in thin coats; these are translucent when wet but become opaque as they carbonate.

Mixing limewash

1. Part-fill a plastic dustbin with clean water, and mix approximately three parts water to one part lime putty.

2. Use a plasterer's whisk fitted to an electric drill to mix the limewash.

3. Test the consistency by dipping in a metal blade. The limewash should be similar to full-fat milk, forming a line along the blade but remaining translucent.

4. For internal use, sieve the limewash using a pair of tights to remove any grit and lumps.

5. If tinting limewash, mix a compatible pigment with hot water by shaking vigorously in a jam jar.

6. Add the pigment to the prepared limewash and mix thoroughly. Test the strength of colour.

Right: As the limewash absorbs CO_2, it converts to calcium carbonate, becoming more opaque and lightening in colour. Limewash is ideal for this timber-framed house, where it is applied over the lime-rendered panels and frame to maximise breathability.

Linseed oil paint

Useful for: external joinery

Linseed oil paint is the original form of oil paint. Applied correctly in a sheltered location it can last over ten years before it needs reapplying. The paints do not contain any solvents or preservatives and are breathable. The linseed is extracted from the seeds of the flax plant, a renewable and sustainable resource. Natural pigments, generally containing no added solvents, are used to provide colour, although titanium dioxide is employed. On external surfaces, zinc oxide is added to the first coat as a barrier against possible mould growth.

The process of applying linseed oil paint is relatively simple but always follow the manufacturer's instructions. The paint should ideally be applied to bare wood as it penetrates the pores of the wood helping to keep moisture out but, where sound historic paint exists, it can be applied over the top. As it dries, linseed oil paint forms a flexible film so is more resilient to cracking than many other coatings. Over time the surface of the paint oxidises, becoming chalky and matt, but the wood remains protected. The downside of linseed oil paint is that it takes quite a long time to dry and must be applied in very thin coats. If applied too thickly, the paint forms a skin and stays wet underneath.

When using linseed oil paint remember:

> Bare wood should be primed with one coat of warmed, purified, raw linseed oil.
> A number of coats will be required and each must thoroughly dry before the next.
> The paint is slow to dry in cold and damp conditions so its application during the autumn and winter is not recommended.
> Faded colours can be revitalised with a coat of raw linseed oil or a single coat of fresh paint.
> There is no need to remove previous coats when applying fresh coats in the future.
> Linseed soap is used to clean hands and brushes.

Top tip: Fire risk

Warning: If you use rags to apply or clean up linseed oil, beware of the risk of fire as they can spontaneously combust. Always dispose of them in an airtight container away from the building.

Above: Applying linseed oil paint to a historic sash window frame.

Above right: Silicate paints can be used for external masonry, but think twice before covering original surfaces as this is invariably difficult to reverse.

Silicate paints

Useful for: external wall surfaces in exposed locations

Highly durable and VOC-free, silicate paints are vapour-permeable and offer an alternative to limewash. Being water-, alkaline- and mineral-based, they are mould-resistant. The paint soaks into substrates such as brick, stone, concrete, pebble dash, plaster and render and, when the water evaporates, natural chemical bonding of the silicate occurs. The structure of the paint allows the passage of vapour but it contains hydrophobic additives that prevent the ingress of liquid water, making it suitable for certain exposed locations where wind-driven rain is an issue.

Soft distemper

Useful for: internal walls and ceilings, particularly decorative plasterwork

Soft distemper was a common internal finish due to its cheapness and ease of mixing. With a velvety, matt appearance, it is a water-based paint generally made by adding hot glue size produced from animal parts to whiting (pulverised chalk). This will create a white paint, but pigments can be added if required. As it dries, the glue sets and the chalk dust creates an opaque layer. To this mix pigments dissolved in water can be added. It should not be confused with oil-bound or 'washable' distemper. These paints are also available from specialist suppliers.

Due to its water solubility, soft distemper cannot be used externally and is unsuitable for damp areas such as bathrooms and cellars where it may become mouldy. It is, however, an ideal paint for ornate plasterwork as it can be washed off before redecorating, hence preventing a build-up of layers which would otherwise spoil the sharpness of original detailing. Despite its beautiful

Left: Soft distempers give a chalky appearance, but their beautiful texture must be balanced against their lack of durability.

Right: Eco paints are also available for woodwork.

texture, soft distemper has largely gone out of fashion, due to the availability of products such as clay paint which are more durable and easier to apply.

Proprietary 'soft distemper' is available ready-made in tins. It is advisable to check the ingredients and additives before buying, as true soft distemper has a very limited shelf-life.

Other eco paints

A wide variety of good-quality paints with eco qualities is now available from specialist paint manufacturers including eco emulsions and those with gloss and eggshell finishes.

These have a variety of characteristics and ingredients, including plant and mineral pigments some claim to be breathable. Before buying, closely question the supplier and obtain a full data sheet listing the ingredients and properties, especially when balancing the needs of the building with eco concerns.

Cleaning up checklist

> With water-based paints, remove as much as possible from tools and brushes before washing under the tap.
> Never pour paint down the sink. Even paints composed of natural ingredients can harm aquatic life.
> Natural paints containing biodegradable ingredients can be left to dry out and then added to the compost heap.
> Take excess paint to a paint collection point.

COLOUR AND LIGHT

Historically, dark colours were used in many interiors, so it is important to decide whether you are going to opt for a traditional scheme or something more contemporary. This has a direct bearing on energy savings. Light colours, and those with a sheen or gloss, make a room look and feel lighter, brighter and more spacious, reducing the need for artificial lighting and allowing lower output lamps to be used. It will also mean that lights can be turned on later in the day.

Below: Limewash has been used to finish these walls, as the masonry and lime plaster is still in the process of drying out. The blotchy effect gives a unique character to the finish, and the pale, subtle shade reflects the light from the window, reducing the need for artificial light.

Choosing paints checklist

When selecting paints and finishes, always try to consider their eco credentials as well as their suitability for the task. Read the label carefully and, if necessary, speak to the manufacturer's technical department to fully understand the ingredients and properties of the product. Remember that a product that works with the building and provides superior coverage and durability is sometimes the better option, even if it is less environmentally friendly.

> Does the coating need to be breathable for the situation in which it is to be used?
> Is it compatible with the substrate?
> How easy is it to maintain: is the finish wipeable or washable?
> Will it be durable, so repeated re-coating and maintenance in the future is avoidable?
> How well does it cover, and how many coats are required to give complete coverage over another colour? What is the coverage per square metre?
> How quickly does it dry? Will longer drying times cause you a problem?
> Is the product biodegradable?
> Is the packaging recyclable or biodegradable?
> Does the manufacturer or supplier take back surplus product to avoid it going to landfill?
> Are VOCs present and if so is the level high?
> Are chlorine preservatives or hormone mimics present?
> Does it contain titanium dioxide?

Below: Some eco paints have a more patchy appearance – this can suit certain interiors but would look inappropriate in others.

Energy and water

Balancing the introduction of the latest energy-generating and water-saving technologies with the needs of an old house is not always easy. Practical thought must be given to ensure any potential gains are worthwhile and not at the expense of the building's aesthetics, structure or historic fabric.

Locally gathered timber has long been burnt in hearths, wind and watermills provided power for industry, while buildings were orientated and designed to maximise the use of sunlight and wind. Today, putting solar panels on the roof may be a very visible sign of being green but is certainly not the most important first step. There is little point in generating energy until the energy use of the building and its occupants has been reduced through measures such as installing insulation, increasing airtightness and using energy-efficient appliances.

There is no one-fits-all solution. What works in a rural situation may not be practical in a city and vice versa. In isolated locations, where mains gas is unavailable and there is reliance on oil or LPG, renewable energy may be an obvious alternative. Even so, it is important not to rush in with quick-fix solutions. First consider the impact they may have on the building and whether planning or other permissions are required.

By considering a holistic approach, which embraces energy and water as well as other measures in the building, it should be possible to avoid inappropriate insulation solutions while still maintaing a comfortable temperature in the house and lowering energy costs and CO_2 emissions.

Opposite: Old buildings such as this Dorset mill have long been used to generate power.

Right: Today, ever evolving technologies are used in conjunction with old buildings for energy generation.

TYPES OF HEATING

Heating systems use a combination of conductivity, convection and radiant heat. The degree to which any of these means of heating is employed will affect your comfort and the efficiency of the house. In reality, the most effective way of heating many buildings is to use a combination of different methods.

Open fires

Traditional open fires such as inglenooks and grates were once the main source of warmth, giving off heat through thermal radiation. The performance of open fires is dependent on a number of factors; in the case of inglenooks, an iron fireback is important to radiate the heat forward. In the past, movable screens, high-backed chairs and settles were used to retain this heat around the area of the fire.

An open fire will inevitably cause a draught as air is pulled through the room and sucked up the chimney through convection. This can easily be observed: the amount of smoke that comes out of a chimney is approximately equivalent to the amount of air being sucked

Above: A traditional open fire radiates heat but creates draughts.

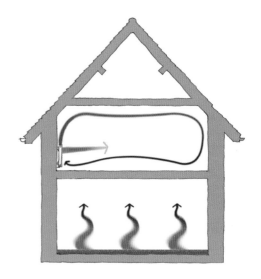

Above: The lower floor has underfloor heating, providing a gentle, constant heat. On the upper floor, a radiator gives off convected and radiated heat.

into the building as a draught. This is countered somewhat by the psychological warming effect of seeing the glow and flames of the fire. Some secondary warming occurs because the surrounding masonry is heated by the flue gases rising up the chimney.

Far left: Open fires radiate heat but tend to be inefficient.

Left: Every open fire needs a working flue, but these are a significant source of heat loss.

Radiators

Warm to the touch due to conductivity, radiators radiate some heat but most of the heat is convected upwards and hits the ceiling before falling as it slowly cools. This makes the upper part of the room hotter than the lower part and causes a draught because the air is constantly moving; as a result you tend not to feel as warm. The problem is exacerbated in many older houses because of high ceilings.

To provide sufficient warmth, radiator systems generally need temperatures of over 55ºC, although low-temperature radiators are available which are capable of working with heat pumps and are useful where under-flooring heating is not an option. Radiators vary hugely in quality and design, so must be chosen carefully to be visually appropriate and to ensure that their performance will match requirements.

Radiators have tended to be fitted below windows to allow their convected heat to warm the cool air coming through the glazing, and because the space beneath a window is not generally used for placing furniture. Where a curtain is then fitted above the radiator, most of the convected heat tends to disappear behind the curtain and out of the window, particularly where the window is not airtight. In some cases it may be sensible to move radiators to internal walls or, where they are fixed under windows, to install a heat reflector behind and a shelf above with the curtain sitting on top.

Inevitably this restricts the curtain length. Bear in mind that radiator cabinets and covers can trap heat and reduce the radiator's efficiency if not designed correctly with well-positioned vents.

Underfloor heating (UFH)

Relying mainly on radiant heat, both electric and wet (hydronic) underfloor systems distribute heat evenly over the whole floor. Typically, underfloor heating makes it possible to lower the average room temperature by 2ºC while still providing an extremely gentle, constant heat and no loss of comfort. From aesthetic and interior design perspectives, it is the least intrusive system as it allows furniture to be arranged without worrying about the position of radiators.

UFH usually operates at around 30–40ºC. This makes it ideal for use with technologies such as heat pumps which provide water at lower temperatures than conventional boilers. The downside of underfloor heating is that it is relatively slow to respond to demand, although this is countered by modern control systems that enable it to be programmed to reach a given temperature at a set time. In the context of an old house, it is the most invasive system when it comes to installation, as it has to be laid into the floor and requires insulation to be installed underneath to ensure the heat is directed upwards. This will result in considerable disruption to the building's historic fabric which may preclude it as an option.

Where a floor has to be replaced, or a concrete slab is being dug up, UFH is a good choice. These systems have been found to be particularly beneficial when combined with the installation of breathable limecrete floors. As the limecrete breathes, the UFH helps to speed up the rate of evaporation of any moisture passing through the floor structure (➡ Solid floors, page 123).

Top: UFH systems often include trays such as this to make installation easier, but these should not be used on breathable floors such as limecrete.

Above: As well as solid floors, UFH can be used under suspended timber floors, but these are not as effective due to lack of thermal mass.

Left: Radiators are often fitted below windows, but consideration needs to be given to their most effective location.

Top tip: Retain the past

Where antiquated heating or water systems are being replaced, pause for a moment to record what is being removed by taking photographs and making notes. Where possible leave the most interesting examples of radiators, pipework and electrical fittings in situ, even if they are no longer serviceable, because they form part of the building's history.

Top tip: Pipe insulation

Fitting pipe insulation needs to be done carefully so every bit of the pipe is covered including joints, bends and hard-to-reach sections. It is a fiddly and time-consuming, but unskilled, job – so ask your plumber whether you can do it yourself to save money and ensure it is done as you want. Always use the best insulation you can afford.

HEATING SYSTEMS

Homes should be maintained at no lower than around 14°C to 16°C. Coupled with ventilation, this will help create an environment with a relative humidity (RH) of 50–70 per cent, which prevents condensation, mould and fabric damage (➡ Moisture and materials, page 44).

Boilers and pipework

Old boilers are notoriously wasteful of energy but before specifying a new model ensure that everything else possible has been done to improve the efficiency of the building, such as installing insulation and cutting air leakage. This means the new boiler can be correctly sized, otherwise it may be unnecessarily large for the job.

Condensing gas boilers are the most efficient option and, where space is tight, a combination boiler is often the answer, but do check that they can be used in conjunction with solar thermal systems if you are likely to consider this option in the future. The same is true of boilers that have a separate hot water tank; ensure both the boiler and tank are compatible with solar systems.

Boilers need a flue and a condensate pipe. Think carefully about how these will affect the building's external appearance and try to ensure they emerge on an inconspicuous elevation. It may be possible to use a redundant chimney stack or other void, although strict rules apply to the installation and inspection of flues carrying combustion gases.

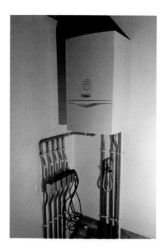

Top: Consider replacing an old boiler with a modern version for maximum efficiency.

Above: Old radiators can be refurbished, and modern reproductions are available.

Left: During refurbishment simplify and upgrade old pipework so it is less conspicuous and more energy-efficient. Check that pipework is correctly sized and try to minimise the length of pipe between the source of the heat and where it is needed. This prevents heat loss from the pipe and, in the case of hot water feeding a tap, minimises the amount of water that is run off and wasted before the hot water arrives.

Right: Boiler flues and vents can easily spoil the facade of a building so their position should be carefully thought through when planning interiors.

Heating control

A key element of any heating system is its control, as this can dramatically increase its operating efficiency. In old buildings, wireless thermostats and controls are a good way of avoiding the need to run cables to various devices and will mean that equipment can be positioned discreetly.

It is important that there is a sufficient flow of air around thermostats and that they are not influenced by draughts or direct heat from radiators. This can be a particular problem where they are enclosed in a traditional-style radiator cabinet.

The efficiency of a heating system is greatly increased by dividing a building into distinct heating zones covering different heating needs. This is particularly relevant in large houses, where only a limited area might be used regularly or distinct areas may be used at different times of the day. This can be accomplished in a variety of ways but is relatively easy using wireless thermostatic radiator valves and a suitable control unit. In some situations additional pipework may be required.

Above: Wireless controls avoid the need for cabling so minimise damage.

CHIMNEYS, FLUES AND FIREPLACES

An open fire can be a good way of building up residual heat in the mass of a building, and should help reduce internal moisture levels. Where flues are to continue in use, it is essential to have them checked regularly.

Background ventilation is vital where combustion is occurring. This would originally have been provided by draughts through leaky windows and doors but, once these have been blocked to make the building more airtight, other means of ventilation must be provided. One option is to fit an air vent in front of or beside a grate to provide a draught at the point where it is required. If such a vent is fitted, consider ways of temporarily covering it to block off the draught when the fire is not in use.

If you have an open fireplace make sure you minimise draughts up the flue when there is no fire. Register grates were invented with a flap at the back for this purpose. Inglenooks can be fitted with canopies with butterfly valves to stop draughts.

When sealing a flue more permanently, give careful thought to ventilating it to prevent damp and rot occurring. This is generally achieved by installing vents both at the top and bottom to ensure a free flow of air through the length of the flue. Special caps that clip over the chimney pot and incorporate vents are available for this purpose.

Left: Leakage of lethal fumes through gaps in brick and stonework and chimney fires are a real danger. If bringing a redundant fireplace back into use, seek expert advice to check the condition of the flue before lighting a fire.

Above: The redundant flue to the left has been capped, but a vent has been fitted to the stack lower down to ensure flue gases do not build up should they escape from the adjoining flue. The right flue has been lined and fitted with a rain-cap and bird-guard.

Another option is to fill the flue. This is a comparatively new and untested solution but offers the advantages of preventing thermal bridging through the chimney stack into internal rooms, is fully reversible and provides a high level of insulation. The flue must be free from damp and should first be professionally swept and checked. The opening at the base is then blocked and the entire length of the flue is filled from the top with a suitable granular insulation such as expanded clay aggregate. The chimney should then be capped. Capping a flue or filling it is inadvisable where other flues in the stack remain in service, as there is a risk that flue gases may leak into it and out into habitable spaces.

It is worth remembering that gas-fuelled coal- or log-effect fires are hugely wasteful of energy and give out very little heat. Installing them is likely to mean that the chimney has to be lined. Always consult a specialist to establish the sustainability of your chimney for any type of heating device that relies on combustion.

Above: Log and pellet stoves are a good way of improving energy-efficiency.

Wood or pellet stoves

Large fireplace openings such as inglenooks are notoriously inefficient and any fire that is lit may be only 20 per cent efficient. One way of improving efficiency, while maintaining the character of the opening, is to install a wood- or pellet-burning stove. These combine the use of a renewable resource with operating efficiencies of around 80 per cent.

Before installation, it is imperative that the chimney is inspected and appropriately lined and insulated to prevent the risk of fire due to raised flue temperatures and increased burn periods. During installation, a metal 'register' plate is installed to seal the gap between the flue from the stove and the larger existing opening to minimise draughts. Some stoves can be ducted so warm air is circulated to other rooms, or they may be fitted with a back boiler so they can be retrofitted to a heating system.

Both wood- and pellet-burning stoves require space for the fuel to be stored. Many pellet stoves, although more efficient and with lower particulate emissions, need electricity to operate. Wood burners can be used in areas controlled by the Clean Air Act 1956, although the stove chosen must comply with DEFRA's strict codes. From a safety perspective, never store fuel immediately next to a stove as the outer casing can get hot.

Fire risk

Any open fire or stove is a potential fire risk but badly installed wood burners in existing fireplace openings are a major concern. A common problem with wood burners is that they are oversized for the fireplace opening or room in which they are fitted. This can lead to heat from the wood burner being so intense that it sets alight nearby timber, such as fireplace lintels, or other adjacent flammable materials.

Research by the National Society of Master Thatchers has shown that more thatch fires are started by poorly installed wood burners than by any other cause. To reduce the risks, the internal stainless steel flue must be insulated properly to avoid hot spots. Always employ an expert and have your flue checked regularly.

Top tip: Chimney balloons

To reduce draughts and heat loss temporarily, a 'chimney balloon' is a good solution when a fire is only lit occasionally. These are available from fireplace shops and are relatively easily inflated

with a pump and then deflated and removed before a fire is lit.

To maintain a small amount of ventilation to the flue it is advisable to trap a short length of tube against the side of the balloon, preventing the chimney from being totally sealed.

Above: If installing a wood burning stove, ensure your chimney is properly lined and regularly checked to avoid fire risks.

Minimising damage

Installing modern services in old buildings can be extremely invasive. Damage to the fabric and look of the building is a big concern, so never leave the planning of an installation to chance. Think ahead and discuss the issues when the work is quoted and with the installer on the day.

> Carefully plan routes for cables and pipes to minimise damage. Wherever possible, try to use existing service routes; redundant chimney flues can sometimes offers a viable passage from the top to bottom of a building.

> Avoid unnecessary or oversized holes, and ensure they are repaired with appropriate materials and sealed against the weather and air leakage.

> Ensure pipes and cables are as visually unobtrusive as possible but avoid chasing into historic surfaces.

> Carefully consider where to site control equipment to minimise its physical and aesthetic impact. Selecting its location carefully may mean that pipes and cables can be routed more sympathetically.

> When several items of control equipment are being installed, mount them on one board to minimise the need for numerous fixings into the wall.

> Wireless thermostats and other control systems offer a good way of reducing cable runs and may be cheaper to install.

> Where trenches must be dug outside the building for cables or pipes, give thought to the archaeology of the site. This is particularly important where ground-source heat pumps are being considered. Trenches dug near existing buildings must be far enough away so that they avoid affecting the stability of the structure.

> Remember that equipment will need to be cleaned and maintained, so try to ensure it is easily accessible to minimise future damage.

> If lifting boards or drilling holes in sensitive fabric, employ a skilled joiner or tradesman to work alongside your plumber, rather than leaving it to chance. Use screws to replace boards that may need to be lifted again or where they are above fragile ceilings.

> Avoid notching the tops of joist to fit new pipes and cables as this will weaken the floor structure.

Far left: Modern technology can be extremely invasive.

Left: Think carefully where items such as inverters are sited. Here, the roof space has been used.

Top: Using a reputable supplier and installer is important, especially where a grant is involved: installers and products recognised by the relevant scheme and with suitable accreditation are a prerequisite.

Above: The size and space taken up by equipment must be allowed for.

Right: Evacuated solar thermal tubes being installed in a discreet roof valley.

ENERGY GENERATION

Once everything possible has been done to reduce the energy use within a building, energy generation is the next consideration. There is a vast amount of information available about the various systems so there is little point in providing exact technical details here, especially as they are continually evolving. What must be thought about are the practical aspects of their installation and use in relation to old buildings.

Aesthetics tend to rank highest on the list of considerations, but damage to the fabric of the building and the ability of the structure to support the technology are equally important. Space to house the associated equipment within the building is a less often appreciated factor, as is the impact of an installation on buried archaeology when digging trenches for pipes or cables, and the disturbance of wildlife such as bats (➡ Wildlife and buildings, page 179).

All systems are likely to require maintenance at some point, so consider how this will be achieved and how future changes may be incorporated without affecting the building. All equipment has a finite life, so it is important to remember that it will have to be removed and replaced in the future. Even if the equipment is in working order, the building behind or beneath may need to be repaired. For example, solar panels might have to be removed to repair a leaking roof. Equally, the installation of a new roof is a good time to consider the installation of energy systems because combining the jobs is likely to be cheaper, less damaging and far less disruptive than adding the technology later.

Often several types of technology are installed to provide a building's energy requirements. If this is the case, it is vital to consider how appropriate they are, not only in terms of their energy output but what their joint impact may be on the building. Look at the scheme holistically to ensure the best all-round solution. Try to procure systems and designs through a single installer or use compatible products from the same supplier to avoid problems with operation or performance.

Solar thermal

Using daylight, solar thermal systems are a means of generating hot water. Two principal types are available: evacuated tube or flat plate. Both systems can be contained within a panel. Evacuated tubes tend to be more visible on old buildings and are potentially fragile so are not suitable where they may be broken by falling branches or missiles thrown at them. Flat plate collectors are more robust and less visible. They have the advantage that they can be integrated into the roof, although this is less easily reversible and means the possible loss of historic roof coverings. Panels may also be mounted on a ground-based array or outbuilding.

If remote from the building, the pipes linking the system must be heavily insulated. The water heated by the thermal panels is stored in a large thermal store (hot water tank) and space is needed to house this together with manifolds, expansion vessels and pumps. The tank's weight must be considered, especially if located on a suspended or upper floor.

Above: A flat plate system on a sandstone-tiled roof in Derbyshire.

tend to be popular because they are relatively easy to set up on a roof; PV tiles and slates are integrated with the roof covering. The majority of these integrated tiles and slates have the disadvantage that they are made to the dimensions of modern machine-made tiles and slates so are only suitable for re-roofing projects using new materials. Whichever option is chosen, consider where the inverter will be sited within the building.

PVs can be located away from the point that the electricity is used, so can be sited on outbuildings or in ground-based arrays. Where a building is not connected to the electricity grid, batteries may be used to store the energy, although they will take up space and need a cool ventilated environment.

Photovoltaic/thermal (PVT)

A relatively new technology, PVT combines solar PVs and solar thermal into one panel. PVT has the advantage that less space is required so it is possible to benefit from both technologies even if the roof is too small to house them separately.

Where a new heating system is being installed and solar thermal is being contemplated as a later addition, ensure that you future-proof by installing a boiler and hot water tank that will be compatible.

Photovoltaics (PVs)

Solar photovoltaics use thin layers of a semiconducting material, usually silicon, which, when exposed to light, generates an electric charge. This electricity is fed to an inverter within the building which converts the direct current (DC) from the PVs to alternating current (AC) for use in the house. Excess electricity is generally exported to the grid and earns an income for the owner of the installation.

There are a number of PV technologies: the two principal forms consist of PVs framed in bolt-on panels or individual PV tiles. Panel systems sit within frames and

Left and below: This in-roof photovoltaic tile system is almost invisible when fitted (see the paler patch above and between the rooflights).

Left: Photovoltaic on-roof panel system.

Roof-mounted panels

Solar panels need to be orientated to make maximum use of daylight so, initially, it might seem that they need to be placed in a highly visible position, possibly detracting from the aesthetic harmony of the building. This is not always the case, as there may be more than one suitable location. Many buildings have hidden areas, such as those below parapets, or between multiple roof slopes; for example, 'M'-style or double-pitched roofs. In all cases, consider the impact of shading from parapets, chimneys and other features as this can have a dramatic effect on output.

Alternative options may be to install the array on the roof of an outbuilding or set up a freestanding array within the garden or grounds of the house. It is worth remembering that, although it is easier to have panels grouped together, they can be split and fitted on different parts of the roof, rather than in a single block. There are a number of other key considerations:

> What is aesthetically most appropriate for the type of roof covering? Panels vary in design, texture and colour and are generally reflective. A particularly visible element is the frame, which is often unpainted aluminium. Inevitably, there may need to be some compromise between the appearance and output of the panels. Aesthetically, panels can look particularly out of place on roofs where slates or stone tiles are laid in diminishing courses, or where pantiles are present, because the panels are too regular and smooth against irregular and undulating surfaces.

> Will the panels be fitted on-roof or in-roof? On-roof panels sit above the roof covering so less of the building's fabric is disturbed and the installation is reasonably reversible, but they tend to show more. With in-roof panels the roof covering is removed and replaced with the panels so they fit flush, as is the case with PV tiles. Although this means greater disturbance to the roof and possible damage to the roof timbers, there is less additional loading because the loss of the tiles or slates partly compensates for the added weight of the panels. With a new roof, this solution may also save money as less of the roof covering is required.

> Is the structure of the roof and the building strong enough to support the weight of the panels? It may be advisable to employ a structural engineer to make an assessment. Where roofs need to be strengthened this may have party-wall implications if the roof abuts another property.

> What are the consequences for the roof covering? The type of fixing required will be influenced by the roof covering and the system chosen. The roof's surface must be sufficiently stable and flat. It is usually necessary to drill through tiles or slates so that a fixing can be made to the rafters beneath; the roof covering will also need to be pierced for cables and

pipework. Remember that moss and lichen growth may build up on the roof in the space beneath the panels, and that any damaged tiles or slates will be hidden from view and difficult to access.

> Does the roof covering pose particular issues? Fixing to thatch is not recommended because of the movement of the thatch over time. With lead roofs it is important to remember that they are designed to expand and contract, so the panels should be mounted on the fixed section at the top third of the lead sheet. In the case of felt roofs, it is advisable to replace the felt before panels are installed.

> Is it possible to avoid fixing into a flat roof? One method of installation which enables solar panels to be installed on a flat

roof without any fixing into the roof is to attach them to specially made boxes filled with ballast. This system has the advantage of being easily reversible and means that they can be moved should repairs to the roof be needed. Wind-loading and the weight of the ballast is an important consideration so this option may not be suitable in all circumstances.

> Is there wildlife in the roof? Bats and some birds are protected so, if they are present, advice may need to be sought before work can start.

> What other dangers might the installation process pose to the building? Windows and ornamentation are vulnerable, especially during the erection of scaffolding, so ensure that adequate precautions are taken by contractors.

Heat pumps

Working on the same principle as a fridge, heat pumps take the heat from the ground, water or air to provide heating and in some cases hot water; certain models, notably air-source, can be reversed to cool the interior of the building in summer. Some will store heat in the ground during the summer so it can be extracted in the winter.

Ground-source heat pumps circulate liquid through a long loop of pipe buried a few metres beneath the ground or in a borehole. A similar system is employed to extract heat from lakes or rivers. Air-source heat pumps extract heat from the air.

All the systems are most efficient with well-insulated, airtight buildings. They produce a stable temperature which is comfortable for occupants and ideal for old buildings. Less heat is produced than with a conventional boiler, so they work best with wet underfloor heating systems or alternatively with special low-temperature, fan-assisted or oversized radiators. Usually a small back-up heating system is installed, especially where the heat pump is being used to heat the hot water system as well as provide heating.

A well-ventilated space is required for the heat pump unit and tank, although this can be sited in an outbuilding provided the connecting pipes are well insulated. While ground-source heat pumps are attractive for old buildings because they are largely out of sight, it is important to be aware of the possibility of disturbance to archaeology when digging the necessary trenches.

Biomass

Biomass is biological material that is used to supply energy. It includes logs, woodchips, wood pellets and waste matter such as straw, which are burnt in special high-performance boilers to provide space-heating and hot water. Biomass may also be burnt in stoves where space is limited.

To make the use of biomass sustainable it is essential for there to be a local supply of fuel. Equally important is adequate dry storage space to minimise the number of deliveries and the carbon emissions made by vehicles. Suppliers may impose minimum deliveries or charge more for small quantities. Access for deliveries is essential so that the fuel can be unloaded close to the point of storage.

Top: Ground-source heat pumps involve considerable excavation.

Above: Air-source heat pumps are more visually intrusive, but less expensive to install.

Below: Wood pellets need to be sourced locally to be sustainable.

Above: A log burning biomass boiler.

Biomass boilers tend to be larger than conventional boilers but installing one in a building previously served by an oil boiler can be an option as it is likely to be relatively easy to swap them over without damaging the building's historic fabric. They are also generally considered to be a practical solution in hard-to-insulate buildings due to their high heat output and the ease with which temperatures can be controlled. The disadvantage can be their size and the fact that they tend to require more care and maintenance than other systems due to the need to remove ash and feed the boiler, but some do this automatically.

A flue is required from the boiler, so its position needs to be carefully considered with regard to its aesthetic impact. It may be that an existing chimney can be used, although this must be lined. An alternative is to house the boiler in an outbuilding, but it is important to be aware of the potential heat loss in transmission, and pipes will need to be buried and well insulated. To achieve maximum efficiency when heating hot water in the summer, it may be worth considering an alternative back-up source of energy.

Micro CHP

Powered by gas, combined heat and power (CHP) units employ an internal engine to generate heat for space-heating and hot water as well as electricity. CHP is well adapted to large leaky houses, as space-heating requirements need to be fairly high for adequate electricity production.

Wind turbines

Wind turbines generate electricity. To work effectively they need to be relatively large and require a clear passage of wind, unobstructed by buildings, trees or landscape. Turbines transfer the strength of the wind through any fixing so the vibrations are likely to put a significant strain on the structure. Mounting on old buildings is not recommended and they should never be attached to chimneys. Noise, aesthetics and their impact on wildlife such as birds and bats within the building must also be considered.

Above: The latest CHP units are similar in size to an ordinary wall-hung boiler.

Below left: A 1kW up-wind turbine generates electricity in a coastal location.

Below right: Hydro-power can involve intervention in historic settings.

Hydro-power

The rivers feeding old watermills potentially offer the opportunity for electricity generation. When undertaking a hydro-power installation it is important to conserve the integrity of the mill's structure, any historic machinery and the surrounding environment. As well as the various legal requirements associated with the abstraction of water, it is vital to consider the stability of the building, the space available for the necessary equipment and potential risk of flooding.

Where a mill is capable of working, or of being renovated to a workable condition in the future, make sure that a hydro-power installation does not compromise the ability of mill machinery to work. In addition, the new works need to be as unobtrusive as possible, or they should be kept separate from the traditional machinery, in order to maintain a sympathetic environment. It is worth remembering that in some cases leats, ponds and weirs will need to be repaired and that these may require considerable ongoing maintenance.

Top: Incandescent light bulbs will soon be a thing of the past.

Above: Low energy compact fluorescent lamps are not always compatible with existing fittings.

LIGHTING

Incandescent light bulbs (lamps) are being phased out in favour of low-energy versions. If you have historic fitments this may pose a problem, especially where the light source is visible. Normally, clear lamps were used in early electric light fittings and many had a distinct shape – the equivalent low-energy lamps rarely have exactly the same profile.

When choosing energy-saving lamps, consider the quality and colour of light they offer. Traditional tungsten filaments provide a spectrum of light not dissimilar to fire or candlelight. As a consequence, the colour of light from a tungsten lamp tends to feel more natural in historic interiors.

Compact fluorescent lamps (CFLs) have been the mainstay of low-energy lighting. CFLs take varying amounts of time to come to full power so tend to suit hallways and landings or the common areas in flats and apartments, which remain lit for long periods of time.

Energy-efficient halogens are another option, useful for bedrooms and living areas. Providing dimmable, crisp, white light, they are available in a variety of shapes and sizes and come to full power instantly.

LED lamps

LED lamps, which use light-emitting diodes as the source of light, are superseding other forms of lighting as they use very little power. Since LEDs have a relatively small output individually, multiple diodes are usually grouped together within an individual lamp. Where you are replacing traditional lamps, bear in mind that LEDs have a very different appearance and their light output is unlikely to have the same quality and colour-rendering. Cheap LEDs can give a very blue light so look for lamps with a warm white quality. When dimming LEDs, ensure the installer does not add resistance to the circuit to achieve this as it will increase energy demand. Instead, an electronic ballast should be used to make dimming possible.

Above: Recessed LED lamp and transformer.

Below: Exterior light and PIR sensor.

Exterior lighting

Consider carefully where to site external lighting to minimise damage to the building's fabric and its aesthetics, both during the day and when it is on at night. Light pollution is a major concern, so fittings that spill light into the sky or neighbouring properties should be avoided wherever possible.

PIR motion detectors will help minimise the time that lights are lit, cutting both light pollution and energy use. For the same reasons, choose energy-efficient fittings such as LED floodlights and the minimum brightness lamp necessary to achieve the required level of illumination. One way of minimising the impact of cables is to use self-contained solar-powered lamps. Floodlighting of buildings needs to be treated sensitively and is always best linked to time switches that are set to avoid overuse

Top tip: Cable fixings

Ideally, fixings for cables should be made into the mortar rather than the face of bricks or stones. Any damage can then be relatively easily patched or repointed if the cable is removed in the future; a hole drilled in a brick is there for life.

Recessed light fittings

Fitting recessed downlighters may weaken fragile ceilings, compromise the fire protection the ceiling offers and allow air leakage, draughts and the passage of moisture. They are also vulnerable to rodent damage. Insulation must not be placed around downlighters because of the danger of overheating, and fire hoods should be fitted. These are made from intumescent material – in the event of a fire, they melt, sealing the hole and preventing the fire from spreading. Some LED lamps are designed to allow insulation to be laid over them but never assume this and, if in doubt, treat them in the same way as conventional downlighters.

Right: Always consider the implications before fitting recessed downlighters.

DIGITAL CONNECTIVITY

Integrated technology allows appliances, lighting, heating, alarm and entertainment systems to communicate with one another. This offers you greater control over all the equipment in your home and the convenience of being able to monitor and operate it even when you are away.

More importantly, integrated technology is capable of making substantial energy savings because of its ability to turn lighting, appliances and other equipment off when not needed. At the same time, the temperature within the house may be regulated so that comfort is maintained but energy is not wasted. The energy savings achieved have the potential to make the payback times for these systems attractive. Installing high-quality integrated technology may be worth considering, particularly in houses where savings are less easy to make through other means, such as where wall insulation is difficult or damaging to install.

Although wireless systems are available, many installers favour hardwired solutions. In some older houses the thickness of walls, large chimney breasts, steel work and even foil-faced insulation materials may block or interfere with signals, including wi-fi internet.

When undertaking refurbishments consider what you might require as it will be easier to install the necessary cabling at this stage, possibly behind insulation materials. Fully integrated systems are most cost-effective if installed when rewiring electrical circuits. The design of the system should be left to a specialist in smart home technology, not an electrician.

Where wi-fi is being installed, additional transmitters may be needed in roof spaces to maintain connections. Ensure power supplies are available and provision is made so the units can be cabled back to a central hub, ideally with direct access to your telephone line.

Top right: Wi-fi transmitters placed strategically ensure whole-house coverage.

Above right: Satellite dishes can be placed away from the main house in an inconspicuous location.

Top tip: Cable ducting

In order to future-proof your home and minimise ongoing damage to the building's fabric, incorporate plastic pipes or ducts with a 'draw wire' when laying floors or undertaking work to walls. This will enable cables to be pulled through at a later date.

VENTILATION

Ventilation is essential when buildings are highly insulated and draughtproofed to ensure moisture is removed and the air is kept fresh, otherwise condensation and mould growth will result. Obviously you need to achieve a balance between preventing these problems and ventilation that expels useful heat from the building, adding to heat losses.

Mechanical ventilation

Mechanical extractor fans are a requirement in bathrooms and usually operate in conjunction with the room light and are then timed to run for a fixed period after the light is turned off. An alternative is an extractor fan activated by a humidistat which overrides the timer and automatically operates the fan when humidity in the room reaches a set level.

Above: Whole-house mechanical ventilation with heat-recovery (MVHR) system being installed.

Present thinking increasingly favours mechanical-extract ventilation systems where fans operate continuously, sometimes with heat recovered from the air being extracted. Often, whole-house mechanical-extract ventilation (MEV) or mechanical ventilation with heat recovery (MVHR) systems are employed. To be efficient these systems need to be used where air leakage is minimised. While they work well in new houses built to high airtightness standards, they are less energy-efficient in older buildings unless airtightness of less than 5 m³/h.m² at 50 Pascals has been achieved.

Typically, whole-house, multi-room, ducted MVHR systems extract damp air from wet areas – kitchens and bathrooms – and use a heat exchanger to remove heat that would otherwise be exhausted to the outside. This heat is then used to warm the fresh, filtered, incoming air which is distributed to the living areas of the house.

Think carefully about where the unit is installed. Ensure there is room for ductwork and consider noise and maintenance issues. The air filters within ventilation systems must be cleaned regularly and replaced periodically to maintain efficiency and prevent a build-up of pollutants. Whole-house MVHR units are bulky but might be accommodated in a dedicated cupboard or in the roof space.

An alternative to whole-house systems are single-room heat-recovery fans. These avoid ducting and whole-house airtightness issues so result in minimal intervention in an old house.

Passive stack ventilation

Natural passive stack ventilation offers an alternative to mechanical systems. It relies on the movement of air resulting from the difference in temperature between the outside and the inside of the house (thermal draught) and the effect of wind passing over the roof (Venturi effect).

Ducting from wet areas runs to an outlet terminal on the roof. As the internal temperature rises due to activities such as cooking or showering, the air flow increases. Wind speed and direction also influence the rate of air flow. Air is brought into the building from outside through vents in living areas.

Sophisticated demand-controlled inlets and outlets are now available which, working without electricity, are controlled by mechanical sensors measuring humidity or temperature, thus minimising heat loss.

Ventilation ducting

The ducting that is used in ventilation systems is often poorly considered. Installing ducting can be extremely destructive in old buildings, causing damage to the historic fabric, so it it is worth considering systems with small-bore ducting which may make installation easier. Remember that flexible ducting is easily torn and the air flow is reduced by its ridged sides and the fact that it is often squeezed around bends and between joists. Likewise, flat plastic ducting may be ill-fitting, with sharp bends causing dust traps; it is also time-consuming to install and wasteful of materials.

Below: Installing ducting in a loft space for an MVHR system.

WATER AND PLUMBING

Water is a valuable and finite resource. Energy and chemicals are used to clean and pump fresh water to our homes and again to dispose of it.

Minimising water use

Old taps are notorious for dripping and leaking, so ensure that they are overhauled and washers are replaced. Traditionally, basins and baths are often large so, if replacing, consider smaller versions which require less water to fill them. Similarly, older toilet cisterns use much more water to flush than their modern equivalents. One way of cutting the amount of water used in these is to put a brick in the cistern or one of the devices offered, often free, by water companies. An important point to note when doing this, or when installing a new low-water-use toilet cistern, is whether the drainage system can work satisfactorily with a lower volume of water.

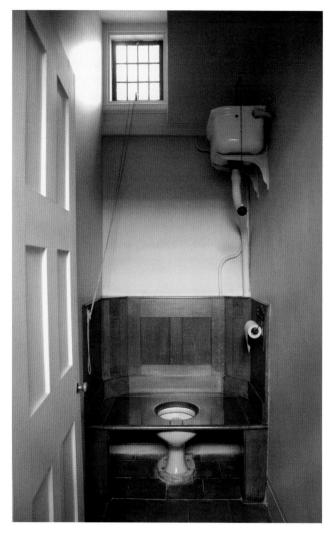

Left: Old cisterns can be adapted for modern use.

Above: Water butts are an easy way of saving water.

Where there is insufficient fall on the drains, debris may not be carried away and blockages can occur. If this proves to be a problem, an inline flushing device can be incorporated underground within the drainage system. This collects a volume of waste water and then flushes it to create a surge through the drain.

Grey water recycling

Grey water systems store basin, bath and shower water for flushing toilets. They are normally reserved for new-build situations as they are difficult to incorporate into existing buildings. Where you are undertaking major refurbishment they may be worth considering, providing their installation does not adversely affect the fabric of the building.

Rainwater harvesting

Rainwater harvesting systems can help reduce rainwater run-off and flooding. The simplest form is a water butt. More sophisticated systems allow rainwater from roofs to be stored and used not only for watering the garden but for flushing toilets, washing cars and even for use in washing machines. They are easier to install in existing buildings than grey water systems but do involve extra internal and external pipework, so care needs to be taken to minimise damage to the building's fabric and appearance.

Space is required for a storage tank either above or underground. Some systems employ a header tank in the loft to which water is pumped from the underground tank. Not all roofs lend themselves to rainwater harvesting, especially if there are many slopes and down-pipes which make capturing the water difficult. The system needs to be sealed to ensure the water does not contain excessive debris.

Sustainable drainage

Water must run away from old buildings quickly and efficiently to prevent damp problems. Where water collects around walls, a French drain is often a good solution; these invariably flow to a soakaway.

Managing surface water has become increasingly important to prevent flooding and the depletion of groundwater. The rainwater run-off from large areas of paving or driveways can be considerable. One way of dealing with this and avoiding the need for surface-water drainage is a permeable surface. Traditional materials such as shingle are ideal. Alternatively consider specially designed permeable paviours.

In some cases these surfaces may form part of sustainable drainage systems (SUDS) designed to mitigate problems associated with rainwater run-off. A wide variety of techniques are used including ponds and storm-water storage systems consisting of buried, hollow plastic crates where water can be temporarily held. When installing these systems, any drainage trenches dug near existing buildings must be far enough away to avoid affecting the stability of the structure.

Below: Ponds can be designed to form part of a sustainable drainage system and are a valuable resource for wildlife.

Left: Water that drains through this retaining wall is able to soak away through the permeable path of slate chips.

Old house for the future

Opposite: Old buildings and good modern sustainable design can happily co-exist.

Below right: Old buildings are a finite resource and need to be cared for if they are to be green.

Sustainability is about more than insulation, airtightness and being energy-efficient. It is not even just about buildings, it is a way of thinking, and often starts with people and communities. Considering the future, and how our houses and environment will be affected, is ever more important in finding the right way forward.

Regardless of any environmental debate, ancient timber-framed cottages and Georgian houses are much sought after while, with a bit of rejigging and modernisation, the Victorian terrace remains the twenty-first-century choice for many families. How we go about making these buildings fit for the future is challenging. It is important to think carefully if they are to be both sustainable and retain the essential essence of what makes them special.

Altering or extending any old building requires a holistic approach. On the route to making buildings eco, what might seem the most obvious path is not always the best way of achieving the greatest gains or retaining the historic context for the long term. There are many things to consider such as the effects of climate change, flooding, rising temperatures, external spaces, biodiversity and the use of appropriate materials.

Repair not replacement is a valuable way of conserving resources. Old buildings are a finite resource and we are duty-bound to ensure that we are able to pass them on for the enjoyment of future generations. There will undoubtedly be a delicate balancing act: costs and gains have to be weighed against comfort and

history. Yet we are entering an exciting and challenging period as we gain a greater understanding of how old buildings perform and can meet the challenges of low-carbon living.

CLIMATE CHANGE

Although it may not seem a priority, we need to consider the long-term effect climate change may have on buildings. Climate change is likely to result in more frequent, severe and unpredictable climatic events and these will increasingly cause problems in the built environment. As well as leading to direct damage to buildings, storms, flooding and intense temperature fluctuations may, over the longer term, lead to the degradation of their structure and the materials used in their construction.

Above: Building materials are likely to be subjected to more extremes of climate.

This is especially likely in the case of old buildings that were not originally built or designed to withstand long-term extreme weather cycles. Higher temperatures, combined with exceptional rainfall, could have an impact on almost every construction material. The stresses imposed may reduce the lifespan of timber joinery and plastics, cause masonry and mortar to crack and increase the likelihood of metals corroding. An inappropriate response to these challenges may put buildings at even greater risk

Rising temperatures

Dry, hot summers have long been recognised as a cause of subsidence. There are also issues associated with the effects of rising temperatures and increased UV radiation on materials, and problems associated with curing mortars and the breakdown of painted surfaces. If winters become warmer, pests such as termites may become established.

Overheating in summer is a key concern and potentially results in significant energy use for cooling. Although a building's thermal mass helps, heat is far harder to get rid of once it is inside, so the first rule is to keep the heat out. While closing curtains or blinds against the sun can help, it tends to trap a layer of hot air between them and the glass which will increase the room temperature. Shading fitted to the outside of the building is the real answer. This is why external shutters, blinds or retractable awnings are a common feature on south- and west-facing windows on the Continent, blocking the heat before it enters the building. In the case of an old building these options may be inappropriate although, where they have been removed, they can be reinstated. To keep heat out it is important that shutters and curtains are closed at sunrise and opened at sunset.

Some buildings are designed with wide eaves to the roofs which help to shade the windows from the high summer sun while still allowing the lower winter sun in to provide warmth. One relatively simple and attractive way of achieving the same result is to build a pergola in front of the ground-floor windows and then to train a vine or other similar climber along the top. This has the great advantage of providing shade in the summer while still allowing plenty of light and useful solar gain to enter the house during winter when the leaves have dropped. Similarly, verandahs can shade the internal area of a house while offering semi-outdoor areas with shelter from the sun and the rain.

A strategically placed deciduous tree is another way of providing natural summer shading, but do ensure it is far enough away from the building to prevent damage to the foundations from the roots.

Right: External shutters are a good way of reducing solar gain.

Far right: Pergolas provide summer shading.

Phase change materials (PCMs)

Designed to deal with the problem of overheating, phase change materials are a high-tech way of adding thermal mass to structures and stabilising room temperatures. They absorb heat during the hottest part of the day and then release the warmth back into the room as the temperature falls at night. This helps to save energy as well as providing increased comfort.

In old buildings PCMs may be particularly useful in loft conversions or attic areas that are prone to overheating. They are generally supplied as lightweight panels laminated on either side with an aluminium sheet. These are screwed or nailed into place behind a plasterboard lining on interior walls and ceilings. Before introducing PCMs into an old building, careful thought needs to be given to the breathability of the structure and the potential loss of original plaster and other finishes.

Cold weather

Frost and heavy snowfall can be hugely damaging to old buildings. Damp walls resulting from poor maintenance or the use of inappropriate materials, such as cement mortars or renders, can suffer frost damage so ensure problems are rectified well before any cold weather. High levels of internal wall insulation that reduce external wall temperatures may increase the risk of frost damage to lime renders. New work involving lime-based mortars and renders should not be undertaken when there is a risk of frost.

Roofs and gutters must be adequate to accommodate any likely snow loading. Snow-guards fitted at the eaves will help reduce the risk of snow or ice falling and causing damage or injury, but can be visually intrusive. Where valley or parapet gutters are present, duckboards or electric heating tape can help keep them clear and allow meltwater to escape without it seeping under the roof covering.

Be careful to prevent salt from coming into contact with the base of walls when paths or roads are gritted – it can lead to the decay of brick and stone.

Storms and wind

The likelihood of an increased frequency of storms and extreme weather events, resulting in tornadoes, hurricanes and a greater threat of thunderstorms, poses a number of risks to old buildings.

Driving wind and rain cause moisture penetration and dampness, which may result in rot and mould growth which in turn may be exacerbated by insulation to walls. The potential for increased lightning strikes means lighting conductors become more relevant and will need to be checked more frequently. High winds and storms also mean that roofs, chimneys, aerials, satellite dishes and technologies such as solar panels must be more rigorously maintained to ensure they are sound and secure. Trees near to buildings need to be monitored to limit the danger of falling branches or uprooting.

Above: Roofs and gutters are vulnerable to the weight of snow and ice.

Above: Unstable and slender chimneys are particularly vulnerable in high winds.

Above: Extreme rainfall events place extra pressure on old buildings.

Below: Flooding poses a real risk to many homes and can come unexpectedly.

Rainfall and floods

Predicted rises in sea levels, coastal erosion, river surges and storms threaten millions of homes with flooding. There is the possibility of insurers limiting or providing no cover against floods in locations that are particularly vulnerable.

Extreme rainfall events and heavy driving rain increase pressure on rainwater and drainage systems and can result in water penetration where roofs, walls, windows and other building elements are defective. Regular maintenance will become ever more important and adaptations may need to be made to handle the increased levels of water.

On older buildings, it is difficult to increase the capacity of rainwater systems without ruining their intrinsic character and detailing, but deeper gutters, more or larger downpipes and greater-capacity soak-aways may be needed to keep the building dry. Flash flooding can occur due to drainage systems becoming overwhelmed by water run-off. Regular inspection and maintenance to deal with problems such as broken gutters, slipped tiles and blocked drains will be even more important.

DEALING WITH FLOODING

If you are unlucky enough to be the victim of a flood, speed but not haste is the key. While there is a temptation to gut the interior and start again, this approach is often unnecessary and results in the loss of period features that may otherwise have been saved. Always aim to keep as much original fabric as possible and clean and repair sensitively to prevent further damage and loss. Remember that the approach promoted by some insurance companies can be highly damaging to old buildings, so seek advice from your conservation officer or other experts with a thorough understanding of old buildings.

Once the building is safe to enter, clear away the water, mud and silt from inside, under floors and from the bottom of external walls. Encourage ventilation by clearing air-bricks of silt, moving furniture and pictures away from walls, and lifting carpets and other floor coverings. With suspended floors, lift a number of floorboards in each room, but no more than necessary, to allow air to circulate, taking extra care to prevent damage when lifting floorboards swollen by moisture. If items such as panelling, door frames and skirting boards have to be dismantled, the work should be done with great care and by a good carpenter. Remember to number and record the position of items as they are removed and turn them regularly to limit warping.

Do not discard items until you are absolutely sure they cannot be conserved. They may in any case serve as a useful model to create replicas or when trying to find matches. Where appropriate, get advice from a conservator, conservation architect or surveyor.

Care and patience is needed when drying out old buildings. Bringing in heaters or turning the central heating to full can be catastrophic, making the remedial process more damaging than the flood itself. The work must be done gently and slowly through natural ventilation such as opening windows and doors and with the aid of fans to help promote air movement and gentle evaporation. Dehumidifiers should be used with caution and, if possible, avoided as they can draw out excessive moisture, causing problems with shrinkage and movement of soluble salts in masonry.

Where windows and doors, including cupboard doors, are left open, be aware of the security risk and, if necessary, fit temporary grilles to secure openings. Stripping non-historic wall coverings will also help the

drying process. Lime-based plasters usually soften when wet but generally harden again when dry. Modern gypsum-based plasters deteriorate when wet and will need to be removed. Allow time for the wall to dry out and then take the opportunity to replace them with lime-based materials as these will cope better with any residual moisture. Be aware that salt deposits, 'efflorescence', may appear. They should be vacuumed off; never wash them as they will be dissolved and re-absorbed back into the surface, exacerbating the problem.

Do not attempt to redecorate until the fabric is totally dry. When you do, it is more important than ever to use traditional breathable paints rather than modern, potentially impermeable finishes.

Mould or fungus growth noticed following a flood is usually only a temporary problem which will disappear once the surrounding fabric is allowed to dry out fully. In the meantime, it is recommended not to use chemical or physical removal systems but instead allow the mould to die naturally. If the problem continues once the building is dry, seek specialist advice with regard to its rectification.

Above: Much of the damage to old buildings after a flood is caused by ignorance in dealing with their repair.

Designing for floods

Although the cause of flooding is often out of your control, there are measures that can lessen its impact:

> Install de-mountable barriers at doors to delay water entering the building, but bear in mind the practical and aesthetic damage they may do to an old building.
> Fit removable air vent and service point covers or wraparound 'skirts', and seal gaps and holes to prevent water ingress, again taking care to be sympathetic to the structure.
> Maintain renders and pointing.
> Install electrical consumer units on upper floors.
> Run all electric cables from ceiling level rather than up from under the floor but be mindful of the potential damage to the historic fabric if walls have to be chased. Position sockets above potential flood levels.
> Fit non-return valves to drainage systems to prevent sewage and foul water entering the building.
> Generally avoid tanking or modern sealants and water-repellent products that trap moisture.
> If replacing a concrete floor, consider a breathable option such as limecrete.

Below: In flood-risk areas, more permanent flood prevention measures may be required.

Above: Good modern design that maximises natural light makes old buildings fit for the future.

DESIGNING FOR THE FUTURE

Respect and understanding are key when working with old buildings. Our built heritage is finite and learning how to adapt it sympathetically is vital. We have already seen what the plastic and double-glazing window salesmen have done to the faces of so many houses, but the consequences of a concerted drive to retrofit buildings without understanding them is a far greater long-term threat.

Extensive research is being undertaken to increase our knowledge of how old buildings and the materials used to construct them behave. New products will emerge and we are going to learn more about how to contribute towards a sustainable future.

In designing for sustainability it is important not to over-complicate things and place reliance on systems and details than can fail if not installed correctly. Simple is generally best, especially when working with old buildings. Buildings must be easy and intuitive to use as well as comfortable and adaptable to changing needs. With an ageing population, thought may be required to make buildings more accessible without damaging their character or how they work.

Passive design

Buildings built to Passivhaus standards are designed to provide good levels of occupant comfort while using very little energy for heating and cooling. To achieve this, high levels of insulation, airtightness and the minimisation of thermal bridging are combined with meticulous attention to detail and rigorous design and construction. This is done in accordance with principles developed by the Passivhaus Institute in Germany.

In new houses, achieving Passivhaus standards is part of the build process. Retrofitting old buildings to the same level is potentially hugely damaging and expensive as it can involve stripping the fabric of the original building back to the masonry walls, leading to much going to landfill.

Interior design and versatility

Houses that are versatile and able to cope with the changing dynamics of family life and an ageing population are increasingly sought after. This is worth bearing in mind when buying or renovating an old building because making it adaptable will allow it to be more sustainable in the long term. Wherever possible, plan ahead so work does not have to be undone in the future which will result in added costs, wasted materials and ongoing damage to the building's fabric.

Always try to incorporate measures that will help save energy and money. For example, traditional clothes-drying racks do not look out of keeping in an old house and are an ideal way of saving on the energy required by a tumble-dryer, the most energy-hungry of all domestic appliances. If possible, site the rack so it can make use of warm air from a south-facing window or a radiator, but do ensure there is sufficient ventilation so the moisture from damp clothes does not cause condensation.

Plan interior layouts so that daylight is used to maximum advantage and energy is saved on artificial lighting. Wherever possible, position the kitchen sink, writing desks and other work areas under or close to windows where they are illuminated by natural light.

EXTENSIONS

Before extending, always think how existing spaces within the building can be better employed. This solution will potentially use fewer natural resources and may be less detrimental to the external appearance of the building. For example, loft spaces are often successfully converted as are basements and cellars, but always bear in mind the limitations of these spaces and the impact this will have on the rest of the house. Rather than putting unnecessary pressure on an old building, a better option may be to create a separate room in the garden. These are often available in kit form or can be built off site and craned into position with minimal disruption. Ultimately, if you move, many designs have the benefit that they can be taken with you.

Careful planning is essential when adding an extension. Consider how the extra space will work with the existing building and how you will circulate within it. It is very easy for the room that an extension is built off to become a corridor, with the result that no real space is gained. Maintaining natural light and ventilation to the existing house is also crucial. Creating rooms that need to be lit by artificial light or ventilated mechanically increases energy consumption and will devalue the 'feel' of the space. Think about installing rooflights or sun tubes to bring daylight into the interior. Staircases and light wells are good ways of introducing natural light.

When building an extension it is worth remembering that it is unlikely to be visited again in terms of upgrading for many years, so always build to the highest specification possible, especially when it comes to thermal insulation and airtightness. Bear in mind that the original structure needs to breathe and, if this is compromised by the extension, damp and other problems may develop. Where an old house has suspended timber floors, ensure that the underfloor ventilation is not blocked (➡ Suspended timber floors, page 129).

Try to design an extension so that minimum damage is caused to the historic fabric of the existing building. This is particularly important when it comes to deciding how to access the new space from the old. If possible,

Top: Drying racks save on the energy that would be used by tumble-dryers.

Above: Loft conversions are potentially a good way of gaining extra space, especially in terraced houses.

Right: These before-and-after shots show how good design can work alongside an old house.

New basements

Digging out a basement under an old house is becoming an increasingly common way of creating more space but there are potential problems. Invariably the new structure is tanked to make it waterproof. While this keeps the basement dry, the displaced moisture may be forced up and outwards, creating damp problems in the walls above. In terraces or semi-detached houses this may have repercussions for adjoining properties, especially in areas with a high water-table. Problems can come about where a terraced property is flanked by newly constructed basements on either side – displaced water may collect under the middle house.

Another consideration is the structural impact on older buildings. Constructing a basement can result in damage and cracking to fragile historic fabric. And because the new basement effectively acts as underpinning, differential movement may occur between adjoining houses where only one has the rigidity created by the basement and the other has shallow foundations.

From an environmental perspective, the disposal of the soil from the excavations should be considered. Lorry movements will be required and the soil might be dumped into landfill.

avoid knocking holes in original walls and instead use existing window or door openings.

Differential movement must be considered. Problems can occur when a new extension with deep foundations is attached to an old building with shallow foundations, so ensure the junction between the two is designed appropriately.

Conservatories

The same issues are associated with conservatories as with any other type of extension but there are additional considerations. By their very nature, conservatories can be too hot or too cold due to the area of glass that they contain, so they may result in high energy use for heating and cooling. Try working with the positives of a conservatory, utilising the solar gain benefits in winter and insulating against the loss of heat at night by shutting insulated doors at the conservatory's entrance into the main building. In the summer, blinds are essential. Conservatories were a Victorian invention so they may look out of place aesthetically with buildings of earlier periods.

Above: This modern take on a traditional conservatory incorporates super-insulated glazing, and provides useful extra space.

Above: With space at a premium within cities, digging down is becoming an ever more popular option.

Extensions: key issues

Think carefully about how an extension can be made to work with the character and architectural rhythm of the original building while being as green as possible in its construction and future performance:

> Consider circulation and how the rooms the extension will be built off will be used in the future.
> Maximise daylight and ventilation into the original building as well as the extension.
> Use green materials that are natural and local.
> Try to achieve the highest levels of insulation and airtightness possible.
> Fit high-performance windows in a style that enhances the original building, rather than detracting from it.
> Think about future maintenance and how areas of the existing building will be accessed once the extension is built.
> Link to the outside so the garden becomes part of the space.
> Add a green 'living' roof.

LOW-IMPACT MATERIALS

Never assume that new work has to be modern brick and block. Many traditional building materials, including timber and lime, have a low environmental impact and some manufacturers have brought them full circle, adapting them to suit today's requirements. These methods of construction can require determination to get them through building control, and builders may have to be persuaded to use and understand them, but perseverance can bring considerable gains in aesthetics, comfort, wellbeing and energy savings. Among the sustainable building materials and products generally compatible with the breathing nature of traditional structures are hemp lime, unfired clay blocks, honeycomb blocks and straw bales.

Left: New extensions should incorporate good detailing and quality materials.

Top: Honeycomb blocks are quick and easy to use and are claimed to out-perform other masonry systems. They offer excellent thermal insulation, a breathing construction and good airtightness.

Above: If properly constructed and kept dry, walls built of straw bales are an excellent building material, offering good thermal properties. Here, lime render is being applied by spraying.

GREEN ROOFS

Constructed over flat or shallow pitched roofs, green or 'living' roofs take various forms, often consisting of sedum or indigenous wildflowers, herbs and meadow grasses. They offer a number of environmental benefits. Importantly, they can increase biodiversity by providing a habitat for wildlife, but they also give visual pleasure; temporarily store water during a storm so its run-off is attenuated to prevent flash flooding; protect the roof-covering from the sun; provide thermal insulation; cut noise and improve local air quality, especially in cities.

Depending on their structure and design, the flat roofs of Georgian and Victorian town houses may be suitable for green roofs, so it is worth considering the possibilities, especially when re-roofing. With old buildings, one of the advantages of some modular green roofing systems is that they are, to varying degrees, removable in the future should it be necessary to put the roof back to its original state.

Left: Green roofs are a good way of increasing biodiversity and can be installed over flat roofs.

Things to consider

Weight is the main issue with green roofs. As well as the dry weight of the growing medium and plants, thought has to be given to the added weight of retained water and snow. On an old roof this may be too much of a strain; think too about wind-loading and address the problem of the green roof blowing off. An assessment by an engineer is essential.

When selecting contractors and suppliers for a green roof installation, it is important to get the necessary level of competence in roofing and horticulture – not all specialists have expertise in both fields. Discuss with them what you hope to achieve: the choice of roof and plant species will influence the type of wildlife it attracts and its impact on the building.

A green roof does not replace the roof covering and there must be a continuous waterproof membrane underneath. It cannot be installed directly on to a metal roof, or any other jointed roof type, as the joints will be vulnerable to moisture ingress by capillary action. Despite the potential thermal benefits of a green roof, additional insulation is still likely to be required.

Although some water is retained by a green roof, gutters and downpipes will be needed to deal with water run-off, and drainage from other existing roofs that runs on to the green roof must be taken into account. It is essential that the growing medium and plants do not block gutters in the future. At the edges, the flashing along parapet walls and around chimneys must be high enough to prevent moisture penetrating the masonry. It is generally advisable to leave a space between the vegetation and the edges of the roof and walls to allow for adequate drainage. This is usually filled with shingle or pebbles.

Access for ongoing maintenance is vital whatever type of green roof is installed. Water will need to be supplied for irrigation if this should become necessary.

Eco roof coverings

If you are extending an old house, consider the green credentials of the roofing materials that you opt for. Thatch is top of the list of eco roof coverings. Locally grown straw or reed is completely sustainable, has very low embodied energy and is fully biodegradable. If detailed properly, it can meet the U-values required without the need for man-made insulation. Hand-split shingle also comes from a sustainable source with low embodied energy, providing the timber is not non-traditional, imported cedar. Shingle is a popular choice with architects looking for a more contemporary roof covering.

Left: Wooden shingles offer an alternative roof covering.

BIODIVERSITY

Over 620 species of lichens have been recorded on built structures in Britain. Buildings and their immediate surrounding potentially provide environments for a huge range of flora and fauna. The decline of some species may be due, at least in part, to the loss of the valuable habitat provided by nooks and crannies in both old and new buildings.

The spaces around buildings can contribute to biodiversity and are important to human wellbeing, particularly in urban areas. Vegetation acts as an air purifier, a carbon store and a food source in the form of nuts, fruits and berries. Trees, hedges and even banks of earth may provide a wind-break or shade and can help reduce the threat of flooding.

Above: Lichens are just part of the biodiversity linked to buildings.

Right: Old buildings are often a haven for wildlife. Monitoring may be required when protected species are involved.

WILDLIFE AND BUILDINGS

Many species are protected by law. Birds, bats, beetles, toads, newts, snakes and snails can no longer be taken for granted. Even a small population of such creatures can stop or slow building work. Ignoring their presence may land you in court.

When a protected species is discovered or suspected, specialist monitoring may be required to gather data to make informed decisions. This may mean re-homing or adhering to seasonal restrictions – for example, by carrying out work only when breeding or hibernation are not taking place.

Bats

All species of bat found in the UK are protected by law. Bats return to their roost year after year, and are found in roofs, eaves space and under hanging tiles or cladding. Signs of their presence include dark brown 4–8mm long droppings which crumble to a powder when dry.

The roost is legally protected, even if the bats do not appear to be there. If work needs to be undertaken that might affect them – including the treatment of wasps' nests, roof repairs, re-wiring or plumbing – you should seek advice at the earliest opportunity from your local Statutory Nature Conservation Organisation (SNCO).

To encourage bats, a variety of bat boxes are available which can be fixed to buildings or built into the structure.

Birds

Buildings are important for a number of bird species, especially the swallow, the house martin and swift, as well as house sparrows, starlings, barn owls and even

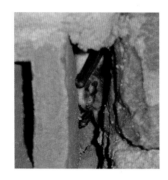

Above: A Natterer's bat roosting in a crevice in brickwork.

Below left: Nesting boxes on buildings are important for birds.

Below: Masonry or mortar bees have burrowed into this cob wall.

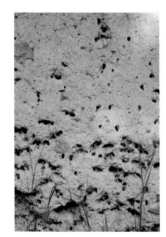

peregrine falcons. In the UK, all wild birds, their nests and their eggs are protected by law. Think carefully before re-roofing or installing insulation that may block entry points and, wherever practical, introduce nesting places. This has to be balanced with the fact that birds can sometimes be a nuisance as their droppings may deface facades and their nests can block essential pipework and flues.

When deterring birds, take the minimum measures necessary and remember that these are sometimes more intrusive that the presence of birds. Fit a cage to the top of the soil stack of the waste drainage system to prevent it being blocked by nests. Chimneys can be fitted with bird guards or an insert. Where birds perching on ledges presents a problem, plastic spikes may be a solution. An alternative is a 'fire gel' repellent – birds see the gel as ultra-violet, making it appear like fire. It also contains natural oils, the smell acting as a further deterrent.

Bees

Masonry or mortar bees burrow through soft mortar joints, stone, bricks or earth structures such as cob walling, usually on the south elevation which has been warmed by the sun. The female constructs tunnels to form brood chambers. The young bees emerge in summer but continue to inhabit the wall until the following spring when they, in turn, make further tunnels. A single bee will not usually cause any significant problem but as the numbers increase over the years the damage may become more severe.

Raking out and repointing, which is best done during late summer or autumn, can deter masonry bees. To avoid damaging the building, a weak lime mortar should be used but this means that the bees might simply return and burrow into it again. Where practical, the solution may be to lay a fine plastic mesh carefully over the area used by the bees each year and encourage them to find a new home. This approach may be required for a couple of summers but eventually does break their cycle.

SUSTAINABLE LIVING

The most eco old house on the planet will fail to meet its full potential if the occupants do not understand how it works and fail to use it appropriately. For example, once air leakage has been reduced in an old building, opening a window in a steamy bathroom becomes more crucial to avoid a build-up of moisture vapour. Equally, developing new habits such as keeping internal doors shut during the winter to minimise draughts within an old house will help to keep energy bills down.

When it comes to retrofitting existing buildings the best solutions are the simplest, most intuitive and well proven. Many traditional materials and construction techniques fulfil these attributes admirably and make subsequent repairs easier.

Sense of place

Communities are central to creating sustainable environments because places with a strong community are good places to live: they are interesting, build human interaction and are safer and more secure. As a result they

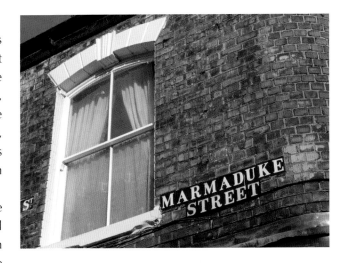

Above: Retaining existing buildings does more than save wasteful replacement, it maintains the traditional urban and rural landscapes and the communities which lie within.

Above: The spaces around buildings can contribute to biodiversity and are important to human wellbeing.

Right: Larger gardens provide an opportunity for ground-mounted solar arrays while drying washing naturally outside saves energy.

tend to be less demanding of resources and wasteful redevelopment is less likely.

The character, layout and grouping of buildings in the past has frequently contributed to a sense of place. Business owners used to live above the shop so did not commute to work over long distances. Traditionally, communities were a mix of ages and were strongly rooted in context, both physical and cultural.

There are many good examples of this. Almshouses and collegiate settings, where the grouping of properties around formally defined courtyards promotes an atmosphere of order, help to balance the occupants' desire for privacy and independence with a reassuring sense of community and security.

Places where people feel secure tend to have longevity and are therefore sustainable. One of the reasons bay windows achieved popularity in the 1870s was that they provided views of the street that were unavailable with ordinary windows. We may associate this with Victorian nosiness but, when it comes to making a neighbourhood safe and secure, the person looking out from a bay window is a far more desirable option than a CCTV camera.

Vibrant places improve economic performance, enhance and support biodiversity, enable healthy living and foster local pride and community cohesion. Importantly, people feel rooted in their surroundings, maintain their homes and know and care about their neighbours. Environmental benefits come from social, interactive processes such as car sharing, local food networks and people working together to grow their own food.

Conversely, soulless buildings that hinder the ability of inhabitants to interact with one another, and that are surrounded by concrete and other hard surfaces with no public spaces, lack a sense of community, are difficult to love and are apt to be less secure. This lack of a real connection to the place in which people live tends to mean that they take less care of it. They might even end up travelling more to escape it, so consume energy, and are likely to move house more regularly, further destroying the sense of community.

Good design coupled with buildings that have retained their character, history and roots bring out the best in human nature, encourage and create convivial places and result in sustainable communities.

Opposite: The Royal Crescent in Bath is a perfect example of the importance of having space around buildings in the urban environment.

Above: Buildings that have retained their character, history and roots, such as this Sussex farmhouse and its associated outbuildings, bring out the best in human nature.

Acknowledgements

Our first and very considerable thanks go to those who made this book happen: Andrew Dunn at Frances Lincoln who enthusiastically took up the idea, Gillian Darley, David Heath and the SPAB Guardians who believed in it and Kevin McCloud who helped sow the original seed. Subsequently Libby Fellingham, with patience and skill, turned unintelligible scribbles into clear and beautiful works of art; Jane Havell painstakingly brought all our efforts together through meticulous editing and design; finally, Marianne Ryan created the index.

Old House Eco Handbook is a joint effort with our SPAB colleagues whose dedicated professionalism has guided the book's contents, particularly Jonathan Garlick, Douglas Kent, Matthew Slocombe and Philip Venning. We owe them all a huge debt of gratitude.

This book could not have been written without the generous contribution and support of the numerous experts who have provided technical guidance on a variety of subjects, as well as access to their own research, much of which is paving the way in this emerging area of science. (The authors accept that any errors in the interpretation of this information are entirely their own.) We would especially thank Paul Baker, Ian Brocklebank, Roger Curtis, James Freeman, Carsten Hermann, Diane Hubbard, Joseph Little, Paul and Angela Mallion, Neil May and Caroline Rye.

In addition, we would like to express our gratitude to a great many individuals who have tirelessly answered questions, provided samples, helped with images, assisted in diagram designs and checked manuscripts. These include: Brian Anderson, William Ball, Justin Bere, Cliff Blundell, Martin Bull, Peter Collins, Bob Cooper, Christof Fehr, John Floyd, Dusty Gedge, Nigel and Joyce Gervis, Antony and Sue Gibbon, Penny Goodchild, Hilary Grayson, Kate Griffin, Sam Hale, Nicholas Heath, Ed Hiam, Mark Hines, Stafford Holmes, Nina Howe-Davies, Philip Hughes, Peter and Betty Hunt, Brett Lane, Sarah Lewis, Ian McKay, Sara MacLean, Liz Male, Valentina Marincioni, Mark Martines, Andrew Mellor, Laura Millbourn, Andy Millmore, Ian Mitchell, Colin Mitchell Rose, Chris Newman, Hugh Osborn, Tony Pensom, Ian Pritchett, Lucy Procter, Ian Randall, Penny Randell, Christian Senkpiel, Eve Setch, Umendra Singh, Andrew Sparks, Martin Spurrier, Robert Squibb, the late Mel Starrs, Alan Stoyel, Mandy Suhr, Tony Swainston, Alan Tierney, Peter Warm, Paul Watts, Katie White, Peter White, Greig Wilkinson, Chris Wiltshire and Adam Wiseman. Huge thanks go to them all and to any we have inadvertently omitted we must apologise.

We would also like to acknowledge the help of all the builders, craftspeople and homeowners who have allowed us to photograph them and their buildings.

Finally, our most heartfelt gratitude must go to our respective partners. Marianne's husband Richard, during the production of this book, has not only tolerated, with exceptional good humour, the disruption to everyday family life, but has also allowed her to experiment with their own home. He has been a wise and knowledgeable sounding board for scientific theory and a great support throughout the process. Equally we owe a huge debt to Roger's wife Elizabeth who persuaded us that this book needed to be written. She did this despite knowing the toll it would take on family life over two or more years. Throughout she has uncomplainingly endured evenings and weekends when 'the book' has been the focus of attention, never failing to encourage, support and advise while being the voice of reason in the face of an ever-approaching deadline. Our sincerest thanks to them both.

MARIANNE SUHR, ROGER HUNT

Picture credits

References are to page numbers

Avonside Daylight 91 left

Baxi 162 top

BBM Sustainable Design 114 centre, 160 top right

bere:architects 34, 113 top, 114 top, 168

Blewbury Energy Initiative 40 right, 41 bottom, 78 bottom left and centre

Built Environment Technology 164 bottom, 165

Changeworks 78 top left and bottom right, 85 top, 157 bottom left

Charnwood 156 top

Clayworks 46

Mildred Cookson 162 bottom right

Glenn Dearing 5

Dimplex 158 centre, 160 top left, 161 centre left

DuPont Energain 171 left

English Heritage/Soki Rhee-Duverne 38 top

FuturEnergy/Allan Graham 162 bottom left

Jonathan Garlick 7 bottom

Historic Scotland 10 right, 18 top, 20, 23, 60 top, 64 top, 86 bottom left, 93 centre right, 113 bottom (both), 117 right, 132 top

Homebuilding & Renovating Show, Centaur Exhibitions 51

Diane Hubbard 42 top,

Roger Hunt 8, 9, 11, 13, 14 bottom left, 15, 16 top and bottom right, 19, 22, 24 bottom, 30 bottom, 31 top, 33 top, 35, 37, 38 bottom, 39 top, 43 top, 44 bottom right, 45 centre, 49 top and bottom, 50 left, 54, 56, 59 right, 62 bottom, 64 centre, 65 bottom, 74 bottom left, 75 top, 76, 78 top right, 80 top, 81 top left and bottom left and right, 82 top right (thanks to Reddiseals), 85 bottom, 86 top (all 4), 87 right, 88, 89 top, 91 bottom right, 92 top left and right, 93 top and bottom (both), 94 bottom,

95 right, 96, 100 bottom (both), 102, 103 left, 104, 106 bottom, 116, 118 bottom, 122, 123, 124, 129, 130 top (thanks to DraughtEx), 130 centre (thanks to StopGap), 131 right, 133, 134, 137 bottom, 138 right, 139 right, 140 bottom (both),141 left, 146, 147 top right, 150, 152 right, 153 centre right, 154 left and bottom (both), 155 top, 156 bottom, 161 bottom left and top right, 163, 164 top and centre, 166 centre, 167, 170 top and bottom left, 171 right (both), 175 left (both), 176 bottom, 177 left, 178 left, 180 bottom (both), 181 top left, bottom, 182, 183

Douglas Kent 17, 25 bottom, 27 top, 39 bottom left, 45 bottom, 71, 136 top, 157 top, 173 bottom, 181 top right

The Landmark Trust 120, 121

Jim Lawrence 94 top

ModCell 177 bottom

NBT 39 bottom right, 139 centre, 177 top

Parity Projects/Chris Newman 26 top, 28 bottom, 33 bottom, 48, 105 right (both) 110 top, 154 top right, 157 bottom right

PEFC UK 31 bottom

Picketts Historic Building Conservation/Alan Tierney 132 bottom, 161 top right

Proctor Group 86 bottom right

PRP Architects 24 top, 106 top, 112, 114 bottom, 151, 158 top, 159 bottom left

Renusol 160 bottom

RSK/Jan Collins 180 top

Caroline Rye 101 bottom left

Matthew Slocombe 50 top, 73

Solar Slate 159 bottom right (both)

SPAB 4, 57, 68 bottom, 84 bottom right, 98 centre, 108 top, 142 top, 152 left, 153 bottom,

154 centre right, 159 top, 169, 172 bottom, 173 top

Christina Suhr 32

Marianne Suhr 10 top left, 14 bottom right, 16 top left, 18 bottom, 21, 25 top, 28 top, 29, 30 top, 36, 40 left, 41 top, 42 inset and bottom, 43 bottom, 44 left, 45 right, 47, 49 right, 53, 55, 58, 59 left, 60 bottom, 61, 62 top, 64 bottom, 65 top, 66, 68 top, 70, 72, 74 top and right, 75 bottom, 77, 79, 80 bottom, 82 top left, bottom left and right, 83 (thanks to TRC Contracts), 84 top and bottom left, 87 left and centre, 89 centre and bottom, 90, 91 top, 92 bottom, 95 left, 97, 98 top and bottom, 99, 100 left, 101 top and bottom right, 103 right, 107, 108 bottom, 110 bottom, 113 centre, 117 left and centre, 118 top (all three) 119, 125, 127 bottom, 128, 130 bottom, 131 left top and bottom, 135, 136 bottom (both), 137 top, 138 left, 139 left, 140 top, 141 right top and bottom, 142 bottom (all three), 143, 144, 145, 147 top left, bottom right, 148, 149, 153 top, 155 bottom (both), 158 bottom, 166 left, 170 right, 172 top, 174, 175 bottom left, 176 top, 178 right, 179

Thermafleece 26 bottom, 63

Thermal Blind Company 81 top right

Timber Design/Cameron Scott 175 bottom right

Tŷ-Mawr Lime 44 top right, 62 centre, 115, 126, 127 top

Mike Wye & Associates/Paul Watts 14 top, 50 bottom right, 67, 105 left

Illustrations designed by Marianne Suhr; reinterpreted, drawn and rendered by Libby Fellingham

Index